REAL ESTATE FLIGHT PLAN

A COMBAT PILOT'S GUIDE TO NAVIGATING REAL ESTATE SUCCESS

REAL ESTATE FLIGHT PLAN

A COMBAT PILOT'S GUIDE TO
NAVIGATING REAL ESTATE SUCCESS

SETH WILSON

#1 Best Selling Author

SWP

SIERRA WHISKEY PROPERTIES

Author's note: The majority of military personnel I worked with in the Air Force are male. While my experience is the same in the real estate profession, I do work with many more women in this field. However, because of the limitations of the English language forcing an awkward use of gender pronouns, I opted to go with the wording that seemed appropriate for the situation, which is normally masculine, and apologize to anyone who feels excluded. That was not my intention.

Paperback ISBN: 978-0-9993932-1-5
Kindle ISBN: 978-0-9993932-2-2

Sierra Whiskey Properties, LLC
SierraWhiskeyProperties.com

Library of Congress Cataloging Number on file with the publisher.

Printed in the USA

10 9 8 7 6 5 4 3 2 1

TO MY BEAUTIFUL BRIDE, DANA LYNN. THANK YOU FOR THE UNENDING ENCOURAGEMENT, STRENGTH, AND LOVE TO ALLOW ME TO BE ABLE TO REACH MY FULL POTENTIAL. I LOVE YOU.

CONTENTS

ONLY ONE WAY TO GO FROM HERE—UP

Tat-tat-tat-tat. Tat-tat-tat-tat. "Hey take a look at that," I announced to anyone who would listen from my seat on the flight deck as copilot.

"What? I don't see anything," the flight engineer replied as he looked out into the ink black of the Iraqi night.

"Put your nogs down," I calmly instructed.

"Oh, shit." Tat-tat-tat. "And look, there's more at the end of the runway about two miles," the pilot pointed out.

What was invisible to the naked eye was as clear as day under the night vision goggles or "nogs"—the unmistakable dashed lines of 7.62-millimeter rounds being shot into the air, dispensed by the venerable and ubiquitous AK-47 assault rifle.

"We have to take off in that direction, toward the gunfire. It's a one way in and one way out runway," I stated as if I was telling the crew something they didn't already know. Takeoff and landing had to happen in the same direction, and that direction was into the rounds being launched into the air.

It was early summer in 2015, and the six-person crew of the affectionately self-named "Herk Team Six" were sitting on the ramp of a small airfield just north of Baghdad, Iraq. The engines were running as we offloaded the cargo necessary to support the Army at their outpost. What was in the cargo boxes, I didn't know and I really didn't care. Whatever the Army needed, we flew it in, and now we wanted to get the hell out of Dodge.

"Well there's only one way to go from here," the pilot said with a tone of authority and confidence. "Up."

Minutes later the throttles were pushed toward maximum thrust and the C-130 "Herk" Hercules took off in the direction of the gunfire.

Pregame Briefing

"Not there again," I thought to myself as my crew of six was briefed on the day's mission two hours before takeoff.

We had been tasked with flying the night mission into the small airfield north of Baghdad. We would take off from our deployed location, a large air base in a small Persian Gulf–coast nation, at sunset, fly an hour and a half to another coalition air base, drop off the passengers that were tagging along, load up with cargo and Army soldiers, and fly another hour and a half to this small unnamed airfield, drop them off, and then fly another two and a half hours or so back to our home base.

The airfield of my dread was a US Army–controlled, Iraqi-operated airfield north of Baghdad International Airport. Which means the Army is running the show, but the Iraqis also have a presence at the field to include air traffic control, and Iraq had helicopters stationed at the field as well.

First off, any place that the Army owns or runs is not a garden destination. It is in my firm belief that the Army intentionally makes their outposts miserable just so they may feel tougher than the other services. Second, this outpost was a complete dump—literally. The town had a large solid waste landfill just on its outskirts.

Flying into this base had some other interesting challenges associated with it. Such as the wire or the fence that separates the airfield from the rest of the town, much the same way the United States has fences around airports. Only this fence is just three feet tall—hardly secure.

Next, our C-130 can only land and take off on the first half of the runway because the northern half of the runway cannot support the weight of the mighty Hercules and is only used by helicopters and other smaller airplanes. This weight restriction forces the C-130 to take off and land in the same direction—to the north.

Landing to the north means that the C-130 must fly low and slow over the low squat buildings of Baghdad, which makes the Herk an easy target for shoulder-launched heat-seeking missiles and anyone with a rifle who wants to take shots at the large aircraft. Taking off to the north has no real consequences except that the runway is half as long as it could be, so maximum effort takeoffs must be performed.

Above and beyond these issues I had little faith in the Iraqi air traffic controllers. I was never completely convinced that they were not working with some cell of Al-Qaeda or ISIS, passing information of our comings and goings or our location in the air so that the bad guys could attempt to shoot at us when we are at our most vulnerable: takeoffs and landings.

That's why this airfield was my least favorite place to fly into—and now to get in and get out of there fast.

Preparing to Land

The most favorable time of day to land at this airfield was at night. The thought was that bad guys would be asleep or not as active and that we could hide the large airplane under the cover of night. While both of these arguments have their merit, in the end I never thought this logic would keep the aircraft or her crew completely safe—there simply were no guarantees.

As we descended into the Baghdad metropolitan area on our flight in, preparing to land, British air traffic controllers gave us instructions on the course and altitude to fly. While this was happening, per local area instructions the aircrew donned our helmets with nogs attached to the top as well as put on our flak jackets with ceramic plates in both the front and back.

The aircraft itself had been modified with its own armor—Kevlar sheets that were laid on the floor and lower windows to prevent small-arms fire from penetrating the cockpit and ultimately the pilots. The airplane was also equipped with classified defensive equipment to defeat enemy missiles. Herk Team Six was as defensive as we could be following all the necessary precautions and checklists.

The Baghdad area was lit up with streetlights and other environmental light from cars and burning piles of trash. Saddam Hussein's former palaces could be easily identified, even from our lofty position, due to their grandeur in both size of the buildings and the expansive amount of Iraqi land the palaces occupied. As we continued to descend toward the airfield, the dark, unlit, winding streak of the Tigris River led us into our destination. Lower and lower we went, preparing the airplane and the crew for the landing.

Each crew member had their sector of the sky to scan to keep a lookout for traffic or hostile projectiles. I scanned to the right when suddenly, "Wham," the entire cockpit illuminated with an intense green glow if only for a second. I was blinded! My night vision goggles went bright green and then to complete darkness. I only had my peripheral vision, and it was dark too.

Within seconds the nogs came back on and all was well again. There was plenty of chatter within the cockpit on what had just happened, but it was clear, as we had been briefed on this before.

Someone with a high-powered laser just shot it into the cockpit—obviously we weren't as invisible as we would have liked. As a safety function, my nogs turned off to protect themselves as well as me. The night vision amplifies ambient lighting more than 10,000 times, so if a laser is shot directly into them, it overwhelms the nogs and they shut off temporarily. Which was highly disorienting to me, but in the end I would rather have the laser hit the goggles than directly in my eye possibly causing permanent damage.

The event had passed, and we had a landing to make in just a few minutes. Actually, the runway was in sight, and I was handed off from the en route British controller to the Iraq terminal controller. The landing was aggressive but safe. The Herk taxied clear of the runway, spun around, and opened the cargo door that is the entire rear of the airplane.

Now it was time for the loadmasters in charge of the cargo and passengers to get them off quickly so that we could be on our way back to our home base. With the short amount of time on the ground and other considerations, we never shut the engines down while the Army accepted their supplies.

Up front in the intentionally dark cockpit, the four of us discussed the blinding laser. After the conversation, I put my nogs back down to look into the black abyss when I saw the dashes in the near sky. After assessing the situation, we understood that it was Friday night, a time that many Muslim couples are married and that the gunfire was most likely celebratory.

But after the excitement with the laser, we didn't want to take any risks of accidentally being shot or just being a target of opportunity like we were to the laser shooter.

During our decision and planning for the departure, an Army Apache attack helicopter formation escorted two Blackhawk helicopters onto the field. Their flight path was erratic and their procedures were foreign to us. They really were a sight to see. The helicopters flew directly over us, which is impolite, and they couldn't have been much more than 80 feet off the ground when they arrived.

The front-end crew ignored them because we had our own tasks at hand and had to trust that the Army helicopter pilots knew what they were doing. When the last Apache was directly above us, the night sky and ground lit up. Night had become day.

"What the hell?" was the most PG thing we shouted into the intraplane radio. The Apache had released flares, the kind of flares that are designed to trick heat-seeking missiles. Our departure planning was interrupted again. We saw flares burning out just a few feet from our plane.

"Let's focus and knock this out," a voice called, bringing the crew back to the reality of our situation and away from the novelty of the helicopters.

The decision-making was quick. We couldn't park the plane overnight here, and we didn't have the gas to let the engines run until the shooting stopped. We had to go.

The front-end crew consisting of the pilot and myself as copilot, the flight engineer, and the navigator all put our heads together to make up a game plan of how we would get out of the area. The plan was to get as high as we could as fast as we could. The pilot gave the broad strokes of how he wanted to exit the airport. The flight engineer ran the numbers to tell the pilots at what speeds the airplane had to be flown to get the most amount of performance out of her. The navigator consulted the charts to find the least populated areas for us to overfly while ensuring that there were no towers or other obstructions that the aircraft could run into.

I would be responsible to handle the radio calls and use some tactical deception in case the bad guys were listening in on our radio frequency, to back up the pilot to ensure he got whatever he needed and ensure he was max performing the aircraft as we left the airfield.

We were all a little rattled, but with a good plan of action going forward, we were ready for the challenges ahead. In just a few minutes the loadmasters would be done offloading the cargo and passengers and it would be time to depart.

With the lights out the much lighter C-130 roared down the short runway heading directly into the very visible gunfire.

"Go," I called in a monotone voice. The pilot pulled back on the yoke and the Herk jumped into the air.

"Gear up," the pilot commanded and immediately made an aggressive right turn to avoid the hazardous area overflying the landfill. In the air the gunfire was much, much closer than it appeared to be on the ground.

"Gear is up," I informed the pilot.

"Flaps up. After-takeoff checklist," the pilot demanded in a cool tone. At no time did anyone on the crew get excited or, worse, panic. At no time was professionalism lost. The crew executed the plan as briefed and did nothing beyond the limits of the aircraft. Was this scenario beyond the experience of the crew? Maybe. Was this situation beyond our capabilities? Clearly not.

As we passed into the higher altitudes and Baghdad had fallen off our right wingtip, in an orderly fashion we all took off our battle rattle of helmets and flak jackets. Not a word was spoken outside of what was required for checklists and radio calls until we finally leveled off at our cruising altitude.

We debriefed ourselves talking about what we could have done better or differently as we exited Iraqi airspace for the darkness of the Persian Gulf. In the end we all agreed that we had done everything as well as could be expected and if we had to do it again we would do it the same way.

The chatter went quiet as we stared out the windows at nothing and everything all at the same time.

Herk Team 6, last flight in Baghdad, Iraq. From L to R: SrA Zach Self (loadmaster), Maj Brian Keatings (navigator), Capt Seth Wilson (co-pilot), SSgt Jacob King (flight engineer), A1C Cody Harter (loadmaster), Maj Tom Kampmeyer (aircraft commander).

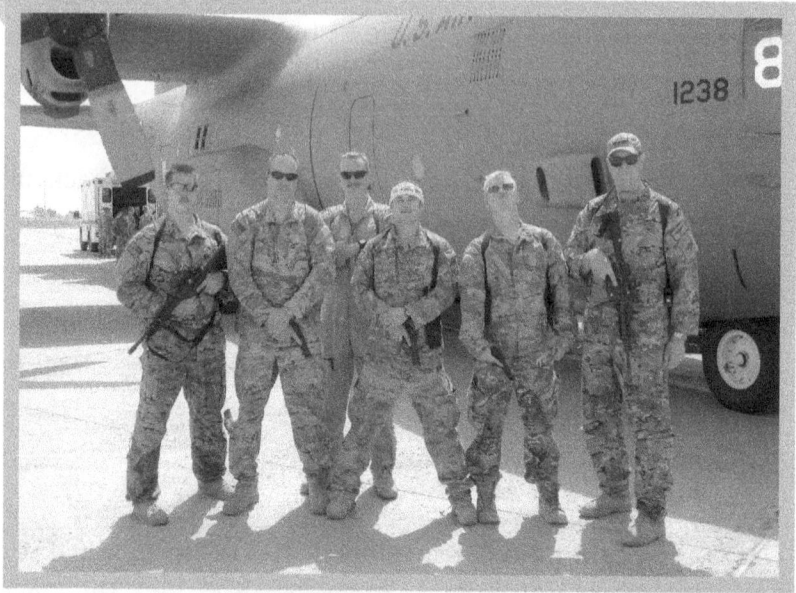

Only One Way to Go

I open with my story about a US Air Force, Missouri Air National Guard C-130 crew that came together with cohesion, professionalism, and even a little bravery. Certainly other books and movies have chronicled stories of the selfless bravery of soldiers, airmen, sailors, and marines in much more harrowing positions than I found myself that night near Baghdad.

Thousands of Americans come back from war and military service with horrible scars both mentally and physically from fighting our nation's wars—and we salute them and especially those who never came back at all.

These stories of heroism and duty all have a common theme—how members of the military can perform at such a high level under unbelievable amounts of stress and confusion and do so consistently.

I use my story to introduce a majority of the themes in this book, such as mission planning, the power of the checklist, leadership (and how to lead with less experience), and knowing that the little details really do matter. Above all, I draw heavily on my military experience to serve in the civilian world with the attributes of integrity (first), service before self, and excellence in everything I do.

This book is composed of a number of easy-to-read, self-contained vignettes that have a simple action-impact-result that has moved me along in my business career. Have I always landed on the centerline, literally in an airplane and figuratively in business? No. And frankly, I share some of those failures as both a pilot and a real estate investor. Why? So you can learn from my mistakes—the ones I will never make twice.

My goal in this book is speak to how you, the reader, can operate at such precise levels set by the military in any endeavor you undertake. Ultimately, however, this book is for three different types of people: real estate professionals, business leaders, and veterans.

For Real Estate Professionals and Business Leaders

Forget the MBA, get away from the classroom, get out of the office, skip the meetings, and see how things are executed in the high-stakes world of combat aviation. I invite you to "fly with me" and take the lessons that I have learned from my more than a decade of military service and internalize them for yourself and share with your firm or company. There is no better way to see situations in black and white than when the decisions that you will make mean literally life and death—and often yours.

As for business leaders, I can't count the number of times I see owners of companies or executives mess something up in a big way when the answer was always so clear to me. I am also sure that if you are a leader who takes the initiative to read this book, you are always on the lookout to make sure that you don't step in what I will politely call excrement. Being a leader is a lot more than taking care of the bottom line, and my hope is that message comes across in this book.

Step outside your comfort zone, strap in, don your battle rattle, and take a seat next to me in the cockpit of this amazing and incredibly small community.

To My Fellow Veterans

I know how tough the civilian world can be. You may have left or be preparing to leave a world of regimen and routine, battle ready and combat hardened, to enter the nasty, dog-eat-dog jungle full of ambiguity and self-promoters willing to step on your fingers at any time for even the smallest perceived gain. In many situations it may seem easier to stay in the military and put up with the BS of those above you and the military system as a whole. Sometimes it seems more comfortable to deploy again rather than separate and try to find a job. Some of you may feel that you don't have anything to offer the business or civilian sector, but let me tell you flat out that you are absolutely dead wrong.

Your service, experiences, discipline, and moral code are what this country needs more than anything else right now. When you read this book, I want you to think about the stories that you have, the things that you have seen, and how those experiences have made you a better warrior and American. Then, armed with your unique story, I want to show you how special you are and how desirable your skill set really is.

I am certain that regardless of your branch, AFSC, MOS, number of deployments, or even performance you have some sort of one-liner that you have internalized such as "slow is smooth and smooth is fast" (not written about in this book) or "Semper Gumby." These types of sayings have a meaning to you that they do not to 99 percent of the population. Even though your military service ends with the DD 214, keep providing "hoorah" or "oorah" (or other primal call) to encourage others, keep adding value to other people and businesses, and you too will quickly find yourself indispensable.

Ready for Takeoff

I graduated dead last in my navigator class in San Antonio, Texas. I really enjoyed my time there, but I was bitter about being there, because I desperately wanted to be a pilot, and didn't put in the time required to excel. I would often show up to mandatory physical training at the crack of dawn not in the best physical or mental condition from spending late nights at the world-famous River Walk in downtown San Antonio.

I had my Air Force friends but I was certainly suffering from the post-college blues as well as a strong resentment about my current station in life. Navigator school was not difficult for me, though, in spite of my poor performance. I had been involved in aviation nearly my entire life so doing things the Air Force way was really my biggest hurdle.

After graduating as a navigator from Randolph Air Force Base, I was assigned to be an Electronic Warfare Officer (EWO) on the top-secret spy plane the RC-135 Rivet Joint. I moved everything I owned in a seven-year-old BMW to Omaha, Nebraska's Offutt Air Force Base. My job was to find, locate, and identify hostile radar systems that would guide deadly radar-guided missiles at friendly aircraft during a contingency or wartime scenario. While I did deploy to the Middle East twice in this role, the missiles never did go flying.

I never truly accepted my fate, and as soon as I saw what the "real" Air Force was like, I wanted to get the hell out of there as fast as I could. But with the fire burning in my belly to become an Air Force pilot, not a navigator or an EWO, I knew I had to focus, to be the best at my job as possible, and to have a good attitude while I did it.

Other than focus, I had to practice or attain other attributes for success. So I modeled myself after others who were successful and asked for their advice. In a short time I was working late, volunteering to lead high-visibility details, and studying my job. Before I knew it, I was ranked very highly in the squadron and had the excellent performance reviews to prove it.

Eye to the Future

While I was busting my butt keeping up the work at the squadron, I had my eye on another prize—to be a real estate mogul. While I was taking a summer college class at Southern Illinois University a few years earlier, the professor was berating my class. The class was Fiscal Aspects of Aviation Management, and I am not, to this day, sure what the class was really about.

But I can still remember almost to the word what he said, and it changed my life: "You all want to be nothing but unionized labor," referring to the majority of the class wanting to fly for the major airlines. "You all just want to fly the heavy iron and screw the flight attendants," he continued. "You need to be reading *Rich Dad, Poor Dad* and other books like that or else you will all get furloughed and will be living in a gutter."

I actually listened to him and read the book *Rich Dad, Poor Dad*. But because I was a broke college student, I couldn't afford the $20 that was required to buy the book. So I sat down in the aisle of the local Barnes & Noble and read the whole thing, cover to cover, while browsers just stepped over me as I digested the financial wisdom of Robert Kiyosaki. That book changed my life forever.

Ever since I was young, I wanted to be wealthy. The challenge was that I was not smart enough to invent something worthwhile, I did not have the silver spoon in my mouth to inherent millions, and I wasn't going to be called up by any sort of professional sports team. So I thought I would just be a pilot and travel the world and live my life out that way—a respectable profession—and I could make a good living. That was—until I read Robert Kiyosaki's life-changing book.

The message is that the wealthy create wealth by purchasing assets and limiting their liabilities. How exactly the rich do this is hinted in the book but is not explicitly spelled out. Kiyosaki leaves the reader to their own devices to figure it out, but he does lean strongly toward real estate.

Real estate? How am I supposed to buy real estate? It is, after all, one of the most capital-intensive businesses on the planet, and I couldn't even afford the book that I was holding in my hands that day at the bookstore.

This is the rest of that story.

FIGHT FOR CENTERLINE

Concentrate all your thoughts upon the work at hand.
—Alexander Graham Bell

Come on use that right rudder," cracked in my headset as I pulled the small four-seat, single-engine Cessna Model 172 back to centerline on a gusty September afternoon.

"You need to get on centerline, you have to fight for it," my instructor, a retired master Air Force pilot, demanded.

"Even all the way out here? We are still four miles from touching down on the runway," I replied inquisitively.

"Yes, even way out here," he sighed.

I was sixteen years old. Barely old enough to drive a car and yet here I was preparing to fly a plane by myself for the first time. The solo is one of the culminating events in any young pilot's life. The solo is when a student pilot with a scant twelve hours or so takes the airplane that they have been training in and flies it for the first time by themselves, no instructors, no passengers, just the pilot and their machine.

The centerline is the white dashed line that bisects the runway and can be seen with the naked eye from miles away on a clear day. To the layman it looks like the center lane divider painted on a long deserted highway. In the aviation world it shows the pilots the exact center of the runway.

The pilot wants to straddle the main landing gear so that in case of any unexpected incident, such as a blown-out tire or a strong gust of wind, that extra room will give the aviator the largest amount of time and pavement to make the appropriate corrections and save the aircraft from running off the runway.

Little did I know that many years later "fight for centerline" would echo in my head again. Not because I was flying an airplane but because I was only a couple weeks away from buying my first $1-million-plus property. Those words "fight for centerline" haunted me as I realized that I had not been on centerline in the months leading up to the closing.

A lot of little corrections from far away from the runway guarantee a good final approach, and a good final approach will set the landing up to be a great landing. I have *never* had a good landing come out of a bad approach. One of the secrets to a good approach is being on centerline as far out as twelve miles. The reason is that the small changes are easy to control and the results of the changes are immediately seen as the pilot gets into the groove of making a good approach.

The pilot can make large corrections close to the runway on final approach, also known as "doing that pilot shit"—words immortalized by Goose in the 1986 summer blockbuster *Top Gun*. In other words, the pilot can make a safe landing after making large corrections at the last moment before touchdown, but finesse and the illusion of mastering their craft is lost. Also as a passenger it is uncomfortable, and this type of action is unnerving to a fellow pilot.

The same is true when it comes to real estate. A real estate company can land on many runways during the course of a property transaction. In my opinion there are three main runways that any real estate firm must land on: the acquisition, the management, and the exit strategy, which most commonly includes the disposition or sale of a specific property. I refer to these three aspects as the three-legged stool.

Exit Strategy

The exit of a property is often an afterthought to less experienced or reckless buyers, but it is always the most important! While the exit is the last action item to occur in a property cycle, it must be the number one, first and foremost consideration, in every purchase. Why? Because to start a project, the end must be in mind. If the leadership team knows exactly where they want to go, they will have a very good idea of how to get there. Not only will this be of great service to the firm when it comes to starting with the end in mind, but it will guide the property and management plan from start to finish.

Each year the company's leadership will know what their goals are and if they have met them; each quarter they will know what the goals are and if they have met them; each month they will...well, you get the picture. The exit strategy guides ownership actions literally every day.

While there are numerous possible exit strategies, at my company called Sierra Whiskey Properties—the phonetic way of saying S and W, my initials—we concentrate on two. We have our primary plan and our secondary plan, if our primary plan can't be executed to our satisfaction in the time frame that we want. Our first strategy is to sell the property on a two- to five-year time line. This plan allows us the horsepower to make large profits faster and more often, also known as the "acceleration of capital."

The second plan is to hold the property and then refinance out of debt that may be of a higher interest rate or of a lower property valuation. The reasons that we could fall back to the refinance plan are numerous but the two largest reasons are these:

- The property is much better positioned in the market than originally anticipated. Therefore, we would want to hold it in a long-term cash flowing portfolio and revisit a sale at a later date.

- The market for selling the property could be poor. It could be a down market and we wouldn't be willing to sell at a depressed price.

Either way we will win as real estate owners, because we took our money and ran to do the next deal. Or we refinanced, took most, if not all, of the initial capital out, yet we still own a great cash flowing property. Now each firm is different and has different investment objectives to satisfy, so the exit plans that we use may not be appropriate for other companies.

The challenge to buyers, without this clarity of mind, is that they think regardless of outside market forces that they will use their one plan and be successful or at least safe. In the mid- and late 2000s, the plan for many people was to ride the appreciation bubble up and up, and then sell to a bigger sucker trying to execute the same flawed strategy. When the bubble popped, some owners got a rude awakening that their plan of simply playing the property appreciation game with no backup was a very dubious proposition at best.

Once again, just because the exit is the last action, never go into a deal without a sound property plan to make the well-thought-out exit strategy a reality.

Acquisition

You've probably heard this cliché: "You don't make profit at the sale, you make profit on the buy."

If an owner overpays for a property, the venture may never become profitable. This is commonsense. However, many real estate buyers fail to think about all aspects of the acquisition process. The deal structure is of critical importance as well. Some questions to think of when purchasing are these:

- How much cash or equity is the buyer coming in with for the deal?

- What are the terms of the debt?

- Is there going to be debt?

- Is the debt interest-only or amortized, and for how long?

- Are there prepayment penalties?

- What is the term?

- Is it loan-to-cost or loan-to-value?

- What are the carve outs?

- What is the rate? How about balloons?

- What is the debt coverage ratio now and in the future?

This is just from the debt (mortgage) aspect, and there are numerous large categories and subconsiderations to attend to as well. As you can see, many consequential issues need to be ironed out before a property is purchased. And this is just purchasing a property that meets all your acquisition criteria. Nothing will sink a deal faster than having a poorly planned capital stack or debt structure that doesn't work for the investor's end goal.

Not too long ago, I turned down a loan that would have sunk the property I was purchasing within a year, and our investors as well as myself would have lost the property and our equity with it. Of course the mortgage broker and the lender tried to push the debt as much as they could by telling us all the ways that we could make the property work for the loan. And that was the flaw. The debt is supposed to work for the property not the other way around. Needless to say, we passed and will never work with those individuals again.

But the cliché is right: money is not made when the property sells but rather when it is bought. The partnership simply realizes the gain when the property is sold. Now let's explore the last leg of the stool.

Management

It can't be said that this is the most important leg of the stool, because all three legs have equal importance, but management really can make or break a property and the people who support it.

To make a confession now: I have never hired a property manager that I haven't had to fire…except one. This confession is to show how serious and stringent I am regarding property management.

The number of reasons why property managers don't work well with owners is long, but the principal reason is because they aren't on board with the diligent owner's exit/property/management strategy.

Some property management organizations are only looking out for themselves and their bottom lines. For management firms to make more and more money, they have to increase their income, which is, of course, an expense for the property and its partnership because the management company's income comes from the partnership. Some of the fees that they charge are simply outrageous. Also, because they are not on board with the property plan in the first place and don't have the same attitude or philosophy that the owners hold dear—integrity, excellence, and service—the third-party property managers don't handle the tenants the way that they need to be treated.

Sometimes tough love is required to get our customers in line. Sometimes the tenants need more leeway or just a couple weeks to get back on track. But all the time we require management to be able to handle them appropriately, and so many property managers, for whatever reason, can't or won't do it.

A New Kind of Management Strategy

Sierra Whiskey Properties has recently taken all property management in house. This management team is led by my brother, Brent Wilson, a University of Missouri business school graduate. Here's how I managed to get him on board.

I had read about scalability of a company or an investment action. I got the idea from Jorge Perez's book *Powerhouse Principles*. Perez is a billionaire real estate developer based out of Miami. After reading his book, I quickly realized that buying one house at a time, fixing it up, and selling it would take me forever to reach my lofty financial goals, and I would never be as successful as Perez.

So I started to gear my thinking toward mobile home parks since I already knew about mobile homes from buying and renting them in Omaha when I served in the Air Force there. It seemed to fit. The issue in Missouri where I had returned to serve in my home state's National Guard was that mobile home parks were, by then, a dying breed. Most cities want to tear them down and build a Walmart.

Once again it came to scale—there just weren't that many of them and the ones in existence were few and far between, so economies of scale in a local area would be hard to achieve. I looked to apartments, specifically B- and C-class apartments, geared toward members of the blue-collar workforce.

I knew I could capitalize on that niche for a number of reasons: First, people are always looking for a safe, clean, and affordable place to live. These types of middle-income apartments are everywhere. And I find there is a huge amount of inefficiency in this market from both buyers and sellers—these inefficiencies could easily be pounced on.

Because a billionaire like Perez got started in his career with this stratum of properties, I decided that I had gathered all the information I needed to jump in with both feet. With no connections, no experience, and no real education on the process of buying this type of investment, I looked for a property that was so surefire that I couldn't miss. Eight months after moving to Kansas City, I found just the property.

The Century Buildings, as they were named, were two Kansas City 6-Shooters. Not knowing what the type of construction was called, I gave them the 6-Shooter moniker because it sounded cool and the construction was prevalent throughout Kansas City. I have seen it nowhere else. The buildings were three-story walkups, meaning no elevator with six units to a building, three on one side of the interior and exterior staircases that bisect the building and three units on the other. Each apartment had a large front balcony.

The property was named the Century Buildings because they were built in 1913 one hundred years before I purchased them for $239,000 in December 2013. The buildings were well built but had seen their share of neglect. Oh, and the property was on the wrong side of the tracks. Well, not railroad tracks, but the buildings were one block east of a north-south street called Troost. Troost had long been the geographical, economic, and racial barrier in Kansas City, but I had not known that at the time and didn't have anyone try to talk me out of buying it. What I did know is that the area had hit rock bottom and had nowhere else to go but up—and I was right.

After about a year of learning the hard facts about the apartment business, I turned the Century Buildings from a property with 50 percent occupancy to 100 percent and raising the rents more than $100 a month. In late 2014 I bought another

Century Buildings. The first multifamily property Sierra Whiskey Properties purchased. Unofficially named "Kansas City 6-Shooter" construction.

undervalued apartment building just down the road from Ford's F-150 production plant.

After I had learned, with the Century Buildings, that most property management firms didn't represent my business philosophies and couldn't keep up with my relentlessness, I recruited my youngest brother, Brent, to become my property manager. At the time Brent was twenty-five years old with no experience with property management at all. He was working as a department manager for Lowe's, in St. Louis, on a slow track to middle management.

I gave him the opportunity to go for something on his own with little oversight and a lot of responsibility. He moved himself, his then live-in girlfriend (now wife), and their two dogs across the state to set up shop in Kansas City. I told him he would have to keep his full-time job because the money managing twenty-four units would not be enough to live on.

So with a tenacity that only the certain fate of becoming destitute could bring, he learned the business from the inside, literally, because he moved into one property and then another as his primary residence. He got to see an aspect of property management that many can never really relate to.

Later he picked up a few single-family houses to manage, and he bought a duplex by living in one side and renting out the other. Finally, he quit his job at Lowe's, and as of this writing manages many units for Sierra Whiskey Properties.

Under Brent's guidance, our management team today is quick to sense changes—then appropriately act. In the local rental market, advertising of the property is multipronged and often at no cost to us to get our properties in front of the right people. We are innovative in receiving payments and in handling other aspects of the property management business. My property managers all are 110 percent on board with the property and management plans, work very well with the tenants and understand the tenants' needs, wants, and desires. Finally, they know that if they take care of the owners' profits, profits will come to them as well.

Feathering My Nest Egg

You may have wondered where I got the cash to buy the Century Buildings. Let me tell you my well-thought-out plan. Well, maybe not well-thought-out, but a plan nonetheless.

I was determined not to let lack of capital slow me down from starting a successful house flipping business when I returned from pilot training in Del Rio, Texas. In order to do this, I had the bright idea of living in a fifth-wheel RV with my dog, Sally. This had a couple of advantages. First, I could live off base, which would give me my full allowance for housing, which was about $1,000 a month. Personnel who didn't live in military housing would get this allowance. Then I would buy an RV for $15,000 or so using 100 percent debt and then sell it back eighteen months later for $10,000 with my actual living expense only being $5,000 for more than a year and a half.

The best part of my plan was to put the RV on base in the family campground that had about twenty spots. So I would actually be living on base but got the money as if I were living off base. This was the beginning of my more-clever-than-lazy planning.

I was hoping my sacrifice living in an RV would pay off, eventually. Actually I sacrificed a lot. For example the RV could only cool the outside air by 20 degrees, which sounds nice until I lived through a nine-month summer in West Texas and the temperature would easily be above 105 degrees every day. And I was living in a tin box.

One of us enjoyed Texas more than the other. Within just a few weeks, Sally became very comfortable in her new surroundings that sat at the edge of civilization and the thick brush of West Texas. If it ran, flew, or slithered, she chased it.

After completing pilot training, I moved to Little Rock, Arkansas, to the unoriginally named Little Rock Air Force Base. I wasn't able to live on base but still got my allowance, so I moved in among my people in a mobile home/RV park in the town of Sherwood.

5th Wheel RV where Seth lived for eighteen months with his dog to save money for his first apartment property.

Once I got back to St. Joseph, the host town of my Air National Guard unit, I was allowed to move into a Holiday Inn. Once again if someone else can pay for my housing and I can pocket the rest, I will do it.

Serendipitously a fellow pilot in the unit introduced me to Ms. Dana Noland during a Mardi Gras party. A few weeks later she asked me out, and two years later I asked her to be my wife while we were on top of a glacier in Alaska.

By the time I left my dwellings in the hotel, I had been saving every dime I could at the personal expense of not having many, if any, luxuries. I had managed to go from less than $2,000 to my name living in my parents' basement to a respectful nest egg of just over $75,000 in twenty-one months of spartan living in an RV and a hotel. Now it was time to put my money where my mouth was and buy a property—and the Century Building was it.

Get Back on Centerline

A couple years later when I was preparing to buy the first property that was worth well over $1 million, there were a number of things that had to be taken into account when the title was about to change hands—the exact same or a similar experience as in flying a plane.

In an aircraft the considerations include weight of the aircraft, wind, weather, visibility, traffic or other airplanes in the area, terrain, and local flying rules, and the list goes on and on. In many cases there are almost as many elements that affect a real estate purchase such as financing, tenant base, title work, surveys, local regulations, property inspections, deferred maintenance, local and national markets, debt, capital improvements to be made, property plan, and investor relations, among many others.

With all of these tasks that need to get done, sometimes in as little as sixty days, a checklist is required and must be strictly adhered to. Many times the checklist items can be accomplished *before* there is even an agreement to buy or sell the property. This kind of foresight is something that will put any real estate firm well ahead of the power curve. When the firm has all its ducks in a row as soon as possible, it makes getting on centerline much easier as the escrow process proceeds to the purchase or a sale. This is the art of making small corrections early in a process so that when it comes time to close a deal, the act is easy, smooth, and almost anticlimactic.

Centerline discipline isn't over once a property is purchased or successfully managed or even sold years later. In the larger sense a firm must always be fighting for where they want to be in regard to their position in their market and their corporate culture, and they must always be fighting for their morals and making prudent actions both internally and in the outside world.

I know firsthand how exhausting a fight for centerline can be day in and day out. A company that I look to as a beacon for this attention to detail and to maintain extremely high standards is a profitable company that delivers an outstanding customer experience. If you've ever experienced the magic, you know I'm talking about Disney.

Disneyland, Disney World, and their other international theme parks deliver once-in-a-lifetime experiences—and rightfully so, some visitors save for years for the opportunity to visit just for a few days. Terminally ill children make it their last wish to see Mickey Mouse in Orlando because it's that special.

Many outsiders and former employees criticize Disney for the high standards that they make employees maintain for the entertainment of guests. Disney simply doesn't care and they don't change the standard because of the pressure coming from critics. Disney knows what works for their guests—they stay on centerline.

Making sure that a real estate firm has the same ambition and tenacity to fight for centerline will guarantee that they will have all the success they can handle.

I don't even have to think about it. When I am in the plane, I always make sure that I am on centerline. As I fly with more and more pilots, it kills me when I see that they are not in a good position to make a good approach and they aren't taking any immediate corrective action to make the small corrections from far away. Then as if a bell rang, the pilot will all at once make large corrections close to the ground and the runway to be in the proper position to land.

Sometimes it works out for them and sometimes is doesn't. I just know I want the odds heavily stacked in my favor for a smooth landing, and I will do anything to make sure that happens—and it starts with being well positioned on centerline.

WAR GAMING
AND OPERATIONS

Coming together is a beginning;
keeping together is progress;
working together is success.
—Henry Ford

In the early winter, cool, gray, overcast skies were the ceiling for Abilene, Texas, home of Dyess Air Force Base located near the center of the state. The only time that I saw this drab scene was during breaks from the long hours of mission planning and briefings that were leading up to the simulated large-scale assault of the Nevada Test and Training Range (NTTR) located north of Las Vegas, Nevada.

Our mission was to take off from central Texas just before nightfall, fly two hours in formation to the NTTR, don our night vision goggles (nogs), descend to 500 feet above the mountainous terrain, and become part of an assault force to violently take a desert airfield from the bad guys. More than 100 different types of aircraft were to each play a part with an important and very specific task to accomplish.

My job on this mission was to keep my C-130 tactical airlift airplane in the number two position with another seventeen C-130s behind me. The line of aircraft was more than fifteen miles long. Onboard each airplane we carried a vital piece of the puzzle for our Army brothers to actually take the airfield.

Our aircraft had members of the 82nd Army Airborne division. Other aircraft had trucks, equipment of an uncountable variety, and even more fully armed soldiers. These Airborne paratroopers would be the tip of the spear when it came to the assault that lay ahead—and there would be friendly casualties.

Back at Dyess the magnitude of the mission that lay head kept us sharp about what we were expected to do, such as coordinating with a large number of other entities in the air and on the ground. The fighter jets would clear the airspace of hostile fighters. The Special Forces on the ground would ensure that the drop zone was as clear as it could be for the Airborne paratroopers to gather and attack. The aerial surveillance would coordinate the airspace to keep friendly aircraft and troops already on the ground away from each other when needed and close together when working in concert. The entire scenario was mindboggling in complexity and scope.

Due to the size of the endeavor, if even one cog of this war machine was not functioning at its highest capacity, the ensuing erosion could mean additional combat casualties and complete or partial mission failure. To make sure that this didn't happen, a small cadre of war planners from each friendly combat entity planned for a week to anticipate every scenario and decided how to pivot if things didn't go as planned. These war planners have earned the title "Weapons Officers"—the result of a six-month crucible that forged them into the experts of their aircraft and how to most effectively use them in combat.

It was then up to us, the rank-and-file, pilots, navigators, flight engineers, and loadmasters that make up the crew of the C-130 to find errors or holes in the plan and offer advice on how to remediate this weakness or to understand the risk if something didn't go our way. Finding issues with a plan that a handful of planners had been working on day and night for a week was easy.

Actually, we reveled in being able to find weaknesses in other aviators' plans—what can I say, it is in our nature. The harder part was fully understanding what we were expected to do for this plan, and if things did go sideways, were we able to make autonomous decisions to complete the mission?

It wouldn't be until late into that night that we would all become fully aware of the singular and potentially fatal hole in the mission that was not planned and would then be so drastically misexecuted that, in this simulated war, real lives would have been in danger of not coming home.

Failing to Prepare

Having a well-thought-out plan is so critical to any venture, it cannot be stressed enough. As Benjamin Franklin said, "By failing to prepare, you are preparing to fail."

Flight planning is one of the most, if not *the* most, important parts of any flight. It's definitely not the sexiest, and it sure can seem boring, however, it is highly important. Crews have a flight plan for painfully obvious reasons: they need to know where they are taking off from, where they are going, what they are carrying in between, and what they will do both on the ground and in the air.

Aircrews need to understand what the weather is going to be at takeoff, en route, and at their destination. Considerations continue not only with obvious, large obstacles but numerous small ones such as fuel management, airspace, traffic, local regulations, temporary flight restrictions, airport closures, navigational equipment being unusable, aircraft performance, and that's just the short list.

All these points and more are addressed in flight planning. Most of the flight planning steps and considerations are difficult to learn and taught via the fire hose effect that I discuss in depth in the next story. Suffice to say, imagine drinking from a fire hose of information gushing at you. You get the picture.

But once the plan is learned and practiced, like all things, tasks become familiar, easy to do, and very rote. What I personally do is create a checklist for flight planning that I maintain. I also continue to add to that checklist, and you'll read more about checklists in an upcoming story. If the checklist isn't working for me, then I add more information to it or change the steps, as required.

A flight planning checklist that I use for the C-130 would not be the same checklist that I use flying a little Cessna single-engine because I won't necessarily have to concern myself with some of the complexities that the C-130 has. The checklists and flight planning would be different based on the different airframes, areas being flown, and what was to be accomplished in the individual flight.

More bad things can happen than good if a flight is not properly planned. An example that I have seen occurred when crews have flown into an airport and then loaded up the plane with gas, passengers, and cargo, and then realized that they could not take off because they were overweight and that would buckle the runway, or because the runway was too short to take off with the amount of weight that they had on board. Then they had to make some sacrifices of gas or cargo—and later do some fancy explaining to their superiors on why the flight wasn't properly mission planned.

Thinking not only about today but tomorrow is the next level of flight planning. The ability to anticipate what events and actions will happen in the future and how to take the appropriate action is a talent very few in the business world succeed with but the ones who do are highly successful in their fields. Sometimes it's easy for information for the future to fall out of the crew's crosscheck.

Crews think, "We're good to go for today," but then they don't think about tomorrow, which would jump up and bite them sooner or later.

Understanding the order of operations that actions need to be completed in, and using a checklist, saves a lot of time not only on the ground but also in the air. For the same reasons crews flight plan, companies must diligently plan their real estate acquisitions and larger projects.

Currently my firm is working on a property that had some drainage issues. To fix these issues there had to be a plan to replace all the roofs and gutters and get water away from the building. Other projects to improve the property include painting, walkway repair, and some other smaller jobs.

The challenge is that if these projects were completed out of order, for example, if the buildings were painted before the roof and the gutters were replaced, then the paint would have to be touched up throughout the property because the gutters would have moved and wood-repaired areas would not have been painted at all. The painters don't mind coming out again and adding their labor and materials to our expenses, but the partnership would be curious why the painting costs were so high. This kind of thinking ahead shows great situational awareness and finesse about an operation.

Execution

Plenty of high-action people and companies charge up the proverbial hill with no plan on how they are going to assemble their actions, who will be a part of the charge, what the challenges will be, what they will do if things don't go as planned, and what the next step will be after they do become successful or how to even know when they are successful and the mission is accomplished. Every logical person can agree that a well-thought-out plan is critical.

But what about taking action? What about the execution?

The execution is what everyone sees. Outsiders never see all the preparation and planning that is involved in making execution successful. Because of this behind-the-scenes preparation, the public thinks that successful companies and people are overnight successes. This simply couldn't be further from the truth. It takes months, years, and even decades to become an overnight success. Dozens of times the person planned, executed, failed, replanned, and reattacked the problem. It was no different in our training for war that night in southern Nevada.

After thoroughly running through the plan, and every crew understood what their part was to be, we launched into the structured plan of execution. Things went perfectly minus some maintenance hiccups on the ground as nineteen C-130s took off into the golden sunlight of dusk.

Once the formation reached a cruising altitude of 22,000 feet, the flight became quite routine. Staying 4,000 feet behind the airplane in front of us was an easy task for a fully qualified crew. As dusk turned to night, the crew became a little complacent and a lot bored having already flown for more than two hours. As we descended the titanic formation to just hundreds of feet above the mountainous terrain of the desert and into the mock war arena, we put on our nogs and mentally steeled ourselves for the dynamic flight that lay ahead.

We approached our drop zone where hundreds of men and thousands of pounds of cargo and equipment were to be airdropped into the drop zone, which is the proper way of saying "throw them out the back of the plane and hope the parachutes work." All I was required to do was stay in position and hold my altitude, heading, and airspeed. I was verbally directed by the navigator where I was to move the aircraft, and

I confirmed his commands with the flight computer next to my right knee.

I must say I was doing a spectacular job. The special operations troops on the ground gave us the winds so we could "gnat's ass" the drop—which is the slang way of saying that we would be so precise with the drop that we could hit a target as small as a gnat's ass.

And then…

"NO DROP! NO DROP!" the navigator shouted in the still of the ebony night, illuminated only by the green glow of the nogs.

"NO DROP, COPILOT," rang out next.

"NO DROP, LOADMASTER," was shouted in quick succession.

"The winds are out of limits," the navigator explained. A no drop is when the conditions aren't right to have cargo or people parachute out of the airplane. In this case the winds were too high for the paratroopers to jump out. Other reasons are varied such as the aircraft may not be aligned properly or the party on the ground has waved us off from the drop.

Now during actual combat, the cargo and the paratroopers would have jumped. Their leadership would have determined that the mission was important enough that they were willing to accept the statistical increase of troops and cargo being blown off the drop zone, as well as the increase in injuries and damage that would have resulted from the strong wind. Alas, we were only training, and there is no reason to jeopardize warriors like that.

So we closed the doors and flew on to the exit point as briefed with all of our now disappointed troopers.

I looked up in the dead of the night and could see the contrails that followed our overhead support F-16 fighter jets. It was beautiful to know that we had their support if any bad guy fighter pilots came to kill our essentially defenseless cargo plane.

And then things went sideways.

Which Way Do We Go?

Due to the no drop, the lead aircraft that was supposed to lead half of the formation to a small airfield just north of Las Vegas was now directed to go to Nellis Air Force Base, which is closer to the city. That would mean that I would be leading the formation; however, I was not qualified to lead the formation and was directed to go to the very back of the formation to hold up the rear.

The maneuver was flown easily enough, and as I rejoined behind the last aircraft, I could see a sight I had never seen before: seventeen other C-130s with their navigational lights bobbing around like small boats on an ocean all trying to stay in position after having already been holding position for the last three hours.

The turbulence from the other aircraft in front of us was horrible—it took everything I had in me to stay in position, full control deflection was needed just to stay upright—so I cheated and climbed above the formation by about 100 feet into the smooth air and relaxed a little. After all, I deserved it and no one would be any the wiser, plus the crew was happy that I wasn't flying in a manner that would make them airsick.

The plan started falling apart fast. The number three aircraft in position was now the lead for eighteen airplanes that were about to break up into three smaller formations and fly off and land at three different bases in the western United States. Needless to say, this new flight leader was not prepared for this responsibility. Why would he be when all he had to do was follow the guy ahead of him?

Now the discreet frequency that was only being used by the C-130s had a lot of chatter on it. The chatter was individual aircraft wanting to break out of the formation and go to their respective bases. Fatigue and restlessness fueled the pilots on the other aircraft to push for a decision when they should have stayed in position and let lead come up with an on-the-spot plan to break the formation into the preplanned pieces.

The lead pilot was not prepared. He did not know who was talking, where they were supposed to go, or the preplanned point where they were supposed to break off. Where was the weapons officer, the one person who could straighten it all out? He was in the aircraft heading to the Las Vegas Strip—I guess he thought his duty was over rather than straightening out the mess he had created.

The new leader succumbed to peer pressure and released the nagging parties. I had eyes on all the airplanes as I was in the rear of the formation. That's when I watched eighteen airplanes break into two smaller formations—one went right, the other went left, both at 10,000 feet.

Uhhh…who do I follow? Who is going to Creech, who is going to Reno, who are you and where are you going? So I stayed in position with the airplane ahead of me.

After a few minutes of a very confused air traffic controller wondering why there were two formations rather than the planned three and one plane just flying by itself to Nellis, I watched a horrific scene unfold in front of me. Two formations of about nine airplanes apiece started to turn toward each other at 10,000 feet even. It is the equivalent of two freight trains barreling head-to-head on the same track. Except these trains are going 200 knots each with a closure rate of 400 knots.

There was essentially nothing I could do other than bear witness to the air disaster about to unfold.

The chatter in the radio went silent as the air traffic controller was now giving very explicit instructions to both formations to turn immediately; the severity of the situation had begun to set in for the other crews. Looking back, had that young airman not directed that turn, the formations would have continued at one another until calamity unfolded. The formations peeled away from one another, and after another fifteen minutes of confusion, the formations were sorted out. The rest of the night concluded without any further challenges.

The plan was sound; the execution was so botched, it could have been fatal.

Indian Ridge Resort

Having a well-thought-out plan that is within the capability of available resources is priceless. Numerous companies, specifically startups, have an idea that develops into a business plan that is then either immediately acted upon or is pitched to investors for capital infusion.

Building a plan requires little human or monetary capital to make. A business plan can be made in the basement of a parent's house on an $800 computer in Microsoft Word. I know because I have done it. The really tough part is the execution, the taking action, the getting out in the real world and making the plan a reality.

In Branson, Missouri, there is an unfinished development of McMansions, called Indian Ridge Resort, that were to be sold for upward of $1 million each. This is a very steep price for a second home in rural, southern Missouri. The development is not on Lake Truman but close enough; the views are good but not great; the real draw to the vacation homes would have been the proximity to rich neighbors.

The entire project was to cost $1.6 billion. The development was so big the governor of the state attended the groundbreaking. This was in 2006. The 900-acre project was planned to include a 390-room resort hotel, a golf course, and a museum and was to have the second largest indoor waterpark in the country.

Only twelve houses were partially completed when the project was abandoned in 2009 and two of the developers sent to prison for bank fraud. Before the fraudsters went to prison, their development company paid $125,000 in fines for violating state and federal clean water laws.

The plan itself was possibly too ambitious for the location; however, the plan could have always been paired down or completed in phases. So the grand vision cannot be completely blamed for the meltdown. The timing was pretty poor as it would not have been feasible for the development to be completed and sold off before the financial crisis of 2008.

Clearly the crystal ball that the developers used had a crack in it—a fatal flaw in the planning. Once again this sort of crisis should have been underwritten, and, of course, hindsight is 20/20, but there was no plan to scale back or mothball the project until economic times got better. The exit plan was single-minded and weak (because this leg of the three-legged stool collapsed), and the development only had one path to success. When that exit door closed, the developers turned to fraud.

The execution, the part that the general public saw, was kicked off in spectacular fashion with a 200-person groundbreaking ceremony with business leaders and politicians in attendance. Later, when the poor execution of construction was combined with the weak plan and then mixed with developers of poor moral character, the project was doomed before it even started.

The end result is that the development today has only a few partially completed and cheaply and poorly constructed houses, and sewer, electrical, and roads were never installed, so the houses stand alone in empty fields.

How could something like this have happened in the first place? How did the development company mislead so many people? How could the execution have been so badly mismanaged? Obviously the developers were liars and willing to do anything to make themselves wealthy.

Then a poor plan was mustered up. I am certain that the projections and the slick brochure that they used to sell the plan were gorgeous and had a wonderfully rosy outlook. Finally, when it came to execution, the developers just couldn't make it happen because they were following their poorly constructed and poorly thought-out plan.

Planning and execution go hand-in-hand with the character of the leader of any venture. The three must be in place all the time, every time, or even the best-laid plans will fail regardless of even the best of intentions.

Moving on Up

After purchasing two properties in two years with valuations that would surpass $1 million within the same time frame, and doubling the equity invested, it was clear to me that I was building something with some value. We had better and better vendors; we were building great systems; and we were ready for bigger properties. The challenge was I didn't know how. I didn't even know of anyone who was in the larger property space. This being the information age, I went looking for a mentor in the first, most logical place: YouTube.

I found Craig Haskell. Craig is a highly successful real estate entrepreneur himself. He has been there and done that. He currently runs a consulting business called the Value Hound Academy that teaches mainly real estate agents and investors how to raise capital, find outstanding deals, organize the syndication of investors, and manage the whole process.

In the winter of 2014 I remember distinctly speaking with him and his outstanding assistant Nikki, seeing their presentation, and knowing that I had to learn what they were teaching to get to the next step in my career. At this point price was not an object. I would have paid anything to get to the next level. The cost of the education was reasonable, and I feel if anything it was underpriced for what I learned and the ongoing support that they continue to provide me.

Using Craig's teachings, I went out to raise money from investors to fund my new, yet undiscovered, acquisition. I was certain that friends and family would be lined up around the block to give me their money to invest for them—I was seriously mistaken. Capital raising was nowhere near as easy as I thought it would be even with Haskell's top-notch training. I kept moving forward, nonetheless, and found a property that was a perfect fit for my investing strategy. It was held by an out-of-state owner. It needed attention and a management shakeup, but best of all it was undervalued.

The 44-unit property located in Riverside, Missouri, was built in the 1950s. Location was ideal because the city had been spending serious money and time to make the river town a great place for families. In addition it was just minutes from downtown Kansas City, and seconds from a large industrial employment base. The property cost $1.5 million—about ten times the amount that I had on hand from the recent sale of the Century Buildings. Undeterred, I called and spoke with everyone that I could think of to raise the money for the sale; I cold called every bank that would take my call. I inspected the building to the smallest detail.

The property was a winner. The problem was that I was not a money-raising winner from either would-be investors or banks. The capital stack was not coming together. After a few months of failure, I wanted nothing more than to throw in the towel and quit. But resolved to sink my teeth in and not let go—I did my best to follow the plan as I did that night during war games trailing eighteen C-130s in the Nevada sky.

I wouldn't give up until the seller kicked me out of the deal. And she never did. I had $350,000 raised to buy the property, which was all the money that I could raise from five investors plus my entire life savings of $150,000.

I was on an Air National Guard trip having dinner on Coronado Island in San Diego, California, when the listing agent called and asked what I wanted to do—this was it, time for an ultimatum. Having had a few drinks in me, I boldly said, "I can only make this deal work if the seller finances the remaining amount." I offered some broad-stroke terms and we ended the call.

Not thinking that the seller would agree to the terms or even the concept, I forgot all about it and flew home the next day. That night I got a call from the broker stating that the seller had accepted my terms and was excited about the prospect of working together. Wow, I went from being sure that I had lost the property to closing on my biggest deal to date about a week later.

The new challenge was that I had the money to buy the property but not improve it. For the next ten months of ownership, we "money balled" the hell out of the property— robbing Peter to pay Paul. In this analogy I was Peter and the property was Paul. It was everything that my brother Brent and I could do to keep the property afloat and make the needed updates. I continued to raise money, but with no new investors I was in a boat without an engine.

In the summer of 2016, I found a firm that saw what we were doing with the property and looked at our track record of success. They took a risk to get us out of the high interest rate note that we had been paying the seller. They also got us the working capital that we needed to upgrade the property so it could meet our property plan and reach its full potential.

Within ten months of the purchase date, the property appraised for $2 million—a 33 percent increase. I also got about $250,000 in cash to make the improvements, which immediately went to good use. The property called Hillcrest Apartments is on a long-term Freddie Mac loan, and we have completed its property plan. The building is a cash cow, exceeding even my expectations and much to the investors' delight.

Lessons Learned

I had developed the Hillcrest Apartments plan in the same way the weapons officers developed their war plan for Nevada. The plan was perfect—on paper. The end was in mind and the starting point was clear—it was the middle part, the management of the plan or the execution, that didn't go 100 percent the way it was supposed to.

While many people may look at both examples and see failure or a plan that went sour, or criticize the people involved, it never helps and only steels my resolve to be better and wiser on the next try. But the way I see both operations is that the people involved fully understood what the end goal was. We all knew where we wanted to be—we just had to take a side road for a while to get there. In both scenarios the event was well planned and the exit strategy was clear: to seize a desert airfield in one case and to buy and improve an apartment building in the other.

In a vacuum the plans would have worked perfectly for both situations, but we don't live in a vacuum. Other people and forces have a say in our plans and actions whether we like it or not. Some are uncontrollable like the winds of Nevada. Some we can control such as raising adequate amounts of capital to buy a building. But either way, if your eye is on the prize, the goal, the finish line, I am confident that one way or another you will find a way to make the dream a reality as long as the tedious job of planning is paired with the unrelenting grind of execution and integrity to inspire others follow your lead.

DRINK FROM THE FIRE HOSE

Risk comes from not knowing what you're doing.
—Warren Buffett

On the first day of pilot training in Del Rio, Texas, the class of 12-11 (a numbering system that identifies classes) was issued a huge stack of reading and studying materials required for the first six months of pilot training. We were preparing to fly the Air Force's primary trainer—the T-6 Texan II. We were also issued flight manuals, numerous navigational charts, aircraft performance graphs, and an assorted amount of other paper products. Stacked on top of each other, the government-issued binders must have been three feet tall.

"This is the beginning of y'all taking a drink from the fire hose," exclaimed the mild-mannered instructor standing in front of the class, with a drawl so typical of the locale.

"In the next six months," he announced, "you are expected to read, learn, internalize, and execute on the documents in front of you to the Air Force's syllabus standards. If you can't, well then, being a pilot isn't for you."

The good news was that we wouldn't have to know it all—that day. But within just a few short months there would be very little in that stack that hadn't been poured over by the thirty students of my class. Six months later we all knew and could execute everything in every one of those binders, and if an individual couldn't, then they were unapologetically dismissed from Air Force pilot training.

I saw numerous broken dreams because of any number of reasons but mostly because my colleagues either couldn't process the information in the stacks of binders or couldn't execute to the exceedingly high expectations of the United States Air Force.

The Air Force is notorious for turning the "fire hose" on its aviators. The fire hose analogy is that the student pilots are expected to learn all the required information all at once and that time is right now. To picture our task, imagine the fire hose that firefighters use to put out house fires, and now imagine trying to take a drink from that flow of water. You would be lucky not to get knocked out let alone quench your thirst.

The catch is that you must at some point drink all the water (knowledge/data/instruction), and you are expected to be able to do it now. There were no bite-sized pieces of information and no visible building-block approach to learning either—you either drank or you perished.

The fire hose methodology of instruction has good reason though, because on the student's very first flight, we were expected to know everything that there is to know about the T-6, the airspace, the procedures, the maneuvers, the grading standards and much more. And why not? Presumably everyone else who is screaming around the flight pattern at 200 knots is also supposed to know exactly what he or she is doing at all times too. The students can kill themselves or others just as easily on their first flight as any other. The standard of performance is set excruciatingly high for a reason—and that is mission accomplishment and safety.

Stack of manuals, regulations, charts, and other pertinent reading materials issued to all Air Force pilot training students on the first day of class. The fire hose was turned on full blast.

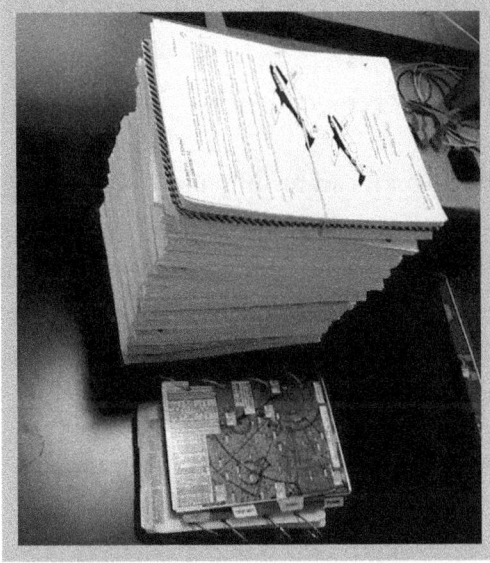

The fire hose of knowledge and data doesn't just exist in the skies above Air Force bases—it is everywhere. I don't need to tell you about how the internet has changed the world or how businesses and people's lives have changed dramatically from the analog way of life and the explosion of knowledge online.

For better, we now have essentially all of human knowledge at our fingertips or at least in our pockets in the form of smartphones. I know for a fact I would not have started a real estate company if it weren't for YouTube, Google, and other unbelievably powerful internet-based tools.

For worse, with so much information coming out of the fire hydrant every moment of every day, it can become very confusing and overwhelming. The sheer wealth of data can stop individuals, businesses, and governments from making critical decisions due to analysis paralysis or just the inability to process all the information to make an informed decision. At any given moment the amount of disturbing video and news, useless junk and other complete time wasters can be streamed real time into your house, your office, and to your cell phone wherever you may be. This all creates a fire hose effect.

Perceive, Process, Perform

In any endeavor, it can be difficult to screen out nonessential data, focus on key facts, and correctly evaluate the resulting risk and opportunities that lie hidden in an overwhelming wealth of information. But the opportunities are there waiting for someone to find them and then capitalize on them. To help in analyzing information, consider these three P's:

- **Perceive** the environment and the market. First, obtain information from reliable sources as well as knowledge gained through previous experiences. Understand that gaining anecdotal information from others experienced in the field can be priceless.

- **Process** the gathered information. This step provides the essential connection between merely obtaining information and doing the right thing with it. The key is an unflinchingly honest evaluation of what the team can do in the newly perceived environment and having a reality check to see if they can take the right steps to act on their objective. Not all combinations of objectives and teams can be successful in every market or environment.

- **Perform** by eliminating or mitigating the risk. Once the information has been processed and its relevance determined, the need to execute the right decision comes next, even if the decision disappoints or inconveniences others. Having some of these decisions made in advance through a predeveloped checklist can be a big help.

I am reminded of a time that I used the three P's in a smooth and logical manner in Canada. Our ultimate destination was Ramstein Air Base, Germany. The C-130 doesn't have the "legs" to fly halfway across the United States and jump across the pond (Atlantic Ocean) and then fly into Western Europe. So the C-130 and her crew stop overnight for crew rest and gas in Eastern Canada before flying to Germany the next day. We awoke early in the morning on the second day of our trip to find that the weather was abysmal in Canada—it was so bad it was almost dangerous to drive let alone fly.

First, I *perceived* the situation. Our mission was to go to Germany to pick up passengers and bring them home. Easy enough. The challenge was that looking out the hotel window we wouldn't have the required weather minimums to take off. We don't get to call a weather day by just looking out the window. So the crew and I packed up our bags and went out to the airport across town to fully assess the situation.

When we arrived at the airport, the loadmasters, crew chief, and flight engineer went out to get the plane ready for its flight while the pilots and navigator stayed inside to *process* the situation and come to a decision. It was true the weather was bad, what we really wanted to find out was how bad would it be and for how long.

We found out that the weather would clear in a few hours, and we would be able to take off. The challenge now was that we had an eight-hour flight to Germany in front of us, and the crew duty day, the amount of time that an aircrew may be on duty, was twelve hours. The clock on the duty day officially started ticking when we got on the bus to go to the airport. This would put us dangerously close to overflying the duty day, which was against one of the ten commandments of military aviation.

Now I could have gotten a waiver to extend our duty day to sixteen hours, but the amount of time and coordination wasn't worth the hassle. I made a time line that was the *perform* aspect of the three P's, that if we weren't in the plane with all four engines spinning at a specific time, that we would abort the flight for today and try again tomorrow.

This decision was moot when the airmen who were preflighting the airplane came in to inform us that the plane was ready to go but there was ice on the wings, even though we were well into the month of May. Flying with ice on the wing is another of the big "thou shall nots" of military aviation.

So I had to go back to the *process* phase to address this new challenge. We would have to get the plane de-iced before takeoff, which is quite a process and costs about $30,000 per application. The challenges were piling on top of each other.

Ultimately, in the *perform* step, I decided to scrap the flight for the day due to poor weather, crew duty day limitations, and the requirement for de-icing. Now, had we been carrying the big bomb that was going to end World War III, then all bets are off and we would have de-iced the plane and launched into the bad weather. But that wasn't our situation, and there was no need to take risky actions like that on routine flights. The crew agreed with the decision, and we all went to Tim Horton's for coffee and donuts on the way back to our hotel.

The Three P's in Practice in Real Estate

The same three P's hold true for real estate. Plenty of people get in trouble time and time again because they have the "I'll figure it out later" or the "that's not important for me today" mindset. The management plan must be solidified before the acquisition. For example, there must be a solid plan as to how the leaking roof will be fixed before it becomes a big challenge, not after.

The only way to protect against down sides and be able to quickly advance is to know what is and isn't important at any given time. This is the same advice that I gave my fellow classmates at Laughlin Air Force Base. What is important right now? Why is this piece of information important? What am I really trying to accomplish anyway?

I ask myself these and a series of other questions to prioritize my knowledge base so I could know what I needed to study and what I needed to do to move forward toward my objectives. In pilot training the objective was simple: to graduate and get the wings that are awarded to all Air Force pilots. In real estate the objective is also simple: to make a number of people and entities as happy as possible for profit and the well-being of everyone involved. The execution is the tricky part.

Kill the Closest Alligator First

In the Air Force we have a saying, "Kill the closest alligator first." This was repeated time and again in training. Which item, event, meeting, appointment, or task is the most important to you in this instant? Which is most important to others right now? Which will prevent you from getting down the line to what you want to be doing next? What will have the biggest consequence if it is not completed right now and delayed until later? This is the event that must be attacked and completed first.

I could write a whole section on this one phrase alone, but let me give you an example from pilot training:

If it was Monday morning, the closest alligator in the flight room was the formal morning brief. This is where we students would sit around the room at attention (yes, you can sit at attention) and one student would give the morning brief to the rest of the class as well as the instructors. Now the dangerous part is that the briefing student may not have seen all the slides that he or she was briefing that morning—there just wasn't time to review everything. The slides were a patchwork from about ten other students putting up-to-date and relevant information and displayed according to the individual instructor's personal preference as to what they wanted to see in the formal brief.

There the student stood, alone and unafraid (sort of), briefing the class and the instructors on the slides that were important to flight operations that day.

If everyone on the team didn't do their small part in assembling that presentation, then the whole thing would blow up—but only on the student doing the briefing. Our colleague who had made the bad slide with incorrect or bad information would be held harmless, minus the resentment of the briefer. This was a perfect example of teamwork making the dream work. But I digress.

The briefing student may have a quiz immediately following the briefing and maybe he studied for it the night before. But also streaming through that student's mind is his prep for a flight later in the day. In the back of his mind he may also have a check ride (or a flight test) the next day that is isn't feeling the most confident about especially the ground part where he will be grilled by his evaluator on any number of topics—which generally means all of them at varying depths.

In this moment the student can't worry about those tasks. He (and a few shes) has to kill the closest alligator first and that is this briefing. He must be calm and focus himself before stepping into the bright lights to brief the class and our instructors using slides he hasn't seen yet today. When things go poorly on stage, he has to be ready to use his previous judgments and experience to help navigate his way through to the logical end—oh, and he has a time limit he must finish within.

After his briefing is over, the class has a quiz to complete. And while the other students are there to help other individuals and get each other to graduation, we are also competitors in the sense that only the top few in the class get the airplane and base that they want—everyone else gets what is left over. So student performance at all times is being evaluated and scrutinized by not only the instructors but also fellow students.

No pressure.

Flying

"I always knew I was going to be a pilot. I just didn't know when," I was quoted saying to a newspaper reporter in Belleville, Illinois, my hometown. I was sixteen years old and had just completed my first solo flight without an instructor in a Cessna 172—a single-engine four-seat airplane. I broke the record for being the youngest pilot to fly alone at Scott Air Force Base. At that time, I had only had my driver's license for a total of three months.

Flying and all things aviation became my lifelong passion. Of course my original plan was to become a fighter pilot and save America, but in the short term, I flew at every opportunity. I advanced quickly in the flight-training syllabus—a little too quickly, it turned out. In the United States one cannot become a licensed pilot until their seventeenth birthday, and since I was still seven months away from that day, I had to slow my flying down from three times a week to once a week.

During one of the intermediate check rides (a practical test performed in the air), I flew as well as someone with thirteen hours in the plane could have been expected. All maneuvers were safe and all parameters flown within. But the evaluator failed me for not using the checklist. What did I need a checklist for? I had memorized all the items on the checklist. Unfortunately, that is not the way it goes, and I had to repeat the ride again the following week—in the meantime, I was devastated. The checklist has become a theme in my life and the next story in this book explains my process in much more detail.

On my seventeenth birthday, I passed my FAA check ride on a gray day in early April and became a full-fledged pilot on the earliest date allowed by law.

Achievement Basis

Sometime in my late high school years, I learned that I was highly achievement oriented. I learned that, much to the dismay of my parents and many educators, I was not interested in incremental gains such as graduating one grade level and going to the next. I was far more fascinated by making big, bold goals and with singularity of focus making them a reality. I have caught plenty of flak for this through the years but not so much anymore as every goal I set has become a reality—maybe not today, maybe not tomorrow, but at some point.

A great example of this was my goal to be an Air Force pilot. I have a framed newspaper article hanging in my hallway with this headline: "Teenager's Love of Flying Gives Lift to His Plans for an Air Force Career." I made the bold statement when I was sixteen that I would be an Air Force pilot. It took me eleven years and a lot of adversity to reach that goal.

Once I realized what truly motivated me in college, it was easy to go forth and succeed without the shame of failure in other areas of my life, specifically traditional schooling. I started my master's degree and did well. I took two classes, got A's in both classes. One day I asked myself, "What are you expecting to get out of this? Are you taking classes because you want to and it will advance you toward your goals, or are you doing this because someone expects you to?"

The next day I dropped out of graduate school.

From then on I went rogue, learning about only the things that interested me and not taking a traditional military career path simply because that is what I was expected to do. Initially, my parents had heartburn about this decision, but once they saw my dedication to my goals and then the fact I was actually achieving them, they took a deep breath and let me spread my proverbial wings.

Drinking from the fire hose was just one more goal and lesson learned that would serve me well whether I was flying heavy iron or buying real estate.

The Stream Continues

The fire hose effect didn't let up at the end of pilot training, flying around West Texas. It continued well into flying in combat zones to include the air above Iraq and Afghanistan.

It was about four days in the air to get from Missouri to the Middle East. The C-130 is not a transcontinental jet. It was designed for shorter flights with the ability to land into remote and unimproved airstrips. Because of this, even when we fly for eight hours a day, we still have only traversed half of North America. Slow and steady really resonates with the C-130 community.

When we finally did land in the desert, after stops in Canada, Ireland, and Greece, we were dead-tired, jet-lagged, and just wanted to get situated in our quarters and relax. Unfortunately, we were in a very hot and dusty climate sometimes insanely humid too, which was not conducive to sleeping or being comfortable. I just did my best to try to get myself organized, find the closest bathrooms, take it easy, and get my bearings on the base that I just flew halfway across the planet to.

The challenge, though, was that the next day, our commanders would direct us fliers to come into the squadron and they'd turn the fire hose on full blast again. We had to learn all about the ATO, which is the Air Tasking Order. The ATO states exactly how the flights are going to be executed, where they'll be executed, and who's going to execute them, and it changes every three days.

Then there are the SPINs—the Special Instructions. The Special Instructions are very dense, hundreds, thousands of pages, of how to operate and fly within the contingency area over the war zone. SPINs also are updated often but generally they are static. However, we still had to learn sixteen-plus years of Special Instructions because they started and are updated from day one of the War on Terror.

Above and beyond the SPINs and the ATO, we also had the ROE, the Rules of Engagement, which spelled out exactly how aircrew will operate when in contact with the enemy or civilians that are not American or allied forces. If contact with the enemy were to happen, the ROE spelled out the different options going forward, and we had better know those backward and forward or risk court martial or, worse, imprisonment by ISIS.

And then, finally, to add to the pile of binders reminiscent of the stack at Del Rio, there was the aircraft-specific information for the base. How we will move the aircraft on the ground, and other local procedures that were specific to operating at our new home base. These were the documents that could get undisciplined aircrew in trouble the most. Because local procedures seemed to be the least threating, some crews didn't understand them as well as they should. But even a small mistake was highlighted because plenty of people at the home base reveled in telling an aircrew why they were wrong.

We also had to familiarize ourselves with the outlying areas, the other bases that we would be flying into, because even though it seemed as if all the bases in the area would follow the same procedures, they didn't. The outlying bases could be run by different countries with a whole new set of rules from the Germans, British, Qataris, or the Iraqi forces, and each host country had a different way of running their base and their local operations on their base.

Welcome to the Middle East, day one.

Aircrews were 100 percent expected to know this potpourri of information and procedures. Unlike flight training in Texas, it was far easier to die, or mess something up, royally, on day one, as it was on day one hundred because there were thousands of people out there who wanted to kill us and our allies—and they would go out of their way to do it too. We had to be diligent about the reality of our situation and soak up every drop from the fire hose.

Expanding the Flow

When I think about the fire hose effect on the real estate side, I think about whenever I want to expand my business into something that the company is not doing right now. For example, if I want to go outside of our business box slightly, if I want to do something other than value-add apartments, I must understand that the fire hose is about to get turned on again.

A good example is on our property management side. It's part of the three-legged stool, as you know, acquisition being the first leg, management being the second, and then disposition being the third leg.

All three legs of the stools are required. With the acquisition side, it's quite easy for us to quickly buy a property. We have been doing it for a few years and have had success with a number of properties. We have our tactics and techniques down on how to make an offer on a property, how to underwrite a property, how to make sure that the property is one that we actually want to own.

The next logical step was property management. We took the information that we gained in the management of our properties, and we realized that we could be doing the community and other owners a disservice by essentially hording our property management company's abilities. We kept our own property management in house, but now we were saying, "You know what? Why are we keeping this to ourselves, when we should be able to expand this in a concentric circle around our core business?"

Such logic made sense. It was complementary to our core business plan to manage other owners' properties for them. So now we're giving owners the opportunity, in our market, to be able to have their properties managed by us in a professional manner.

The challenge for us was the marketing. We had never done marketing for a property management company. How do we get the word out about what we're doing? How do we work the techniques to just talk to these property owners, to find them, to tell them about what we're doing, and how we're going to do it, and then work with them going forward into the future? These were all new questions that needed answers, and they needed answers and action right now!

We understood that there was going to be a fire hose effect to learn all this information. I would learn as much as I could about the techniques and processes of marketing a property management company, getting smart on all aspects, and then going forth to other owners, learning how to speak with them, and asking what they wanted.

Finally we gave them the product and service that they desired, which was high quality and full service. We reached beyond just property management; we also offered referrals for debt, equity, vendors, insurance, brokerage—and all the rest of the teams that are required to make a property a success.

We understood that there was going to be a fire hose effect to learn how to assemble an effective management company. Online sources and social media affirm the seemingly endless opinions and talking heads. Some of them are good. Some of them are not good. Even after we absorbed the information that was available—and drank deeply from the fire hose—we still blended what we learned with our personal style, and how we wanted our clients to be treated.

Once we actually land the client, we create a system of how we report to them, how we pay them. We decide how to deliver some sort of after-action report to communicate what we did, why we did it, and why they weren't looped in if an action needed to be taken immediately. Most owners aren't interested in this sort of detailed reporting, but it is important for us to have processes in place so all actions are above board.

We want to be so streamlined that we have taken care of all property concerns and the only questions the owners need to contact us about are personal or one-offs. We can provide this type of comprehensive communication plan because we are drinking from the fire hose when it comes to adding property management to our portfolio of services. We are making the process seamless, going forward.

Kink in the Hose

The kink in the hose will almost always come from the individual who needs to learn as much as possible as fast as possible. They won't be successful using the fire hose if they are lazy or unmotivated. Or think they can't do it.

Consider this: I have never seen anyone who is *dedicated* to learning as much as they can as fast as they can and then implement their teachings not be successful, sooner or later, in reaching their goals.

The hardest part about the fire hose effect is getting in the right mindset to be ready to accept the challenges that lie ahead and knowing that in the end the drenching from the fire hose of knowledge will be worth it. It is easy to succeed once the fire hose phenomenon is understood and the embarrassment of failure is expelled from the list of concerns. And don't forget that no one is going to shoot your plane down if you don't get it on the first try.

USE THE CHECKLIST

I woke up an hour before I was
supposed to, and started going over
the mental checklist: where do I go from here, what do I do?
I don't remember eating anything at all, just going through
the physical, getting into the suit. We practiced that so
much, it was all rote.
—Alan Shepard

The final phase of aircraft evaluations for the US Army Air Corps was to begin. Three manufacturers had submitted aircraft for testing. Martin submitted the Model 146, Douglas the DB-1, and Boeing the Model 299.

Boeing's entry had swept all the evaluations, figuratively flying circles around the competition. Boeing Corporation's gleaming aluminum-alloy Model 299 had trounced the designs of Martin and Douglas. Boeing's plane could carry five times as many bombs as the Army had requested; it could fly faster than previous bombers, and almost twice as far. Many considered these final evaluations mere formalities. Talk was of an order for between 185 and 220 aircraft. Boeing executives were excited because a major sale would save the company.

At the controls of Boeing's Model 299 in 1935 were two Army aviators. Major Ployer Hill was the pilot with Lieutenant Donald Putt the copilot. Riding along with them was Leslie Tower, the chief test pilot for Boeing; C.W. Benton, a mechanic; and Henry Igo, a representative for the engine manufacturer.

The aircraft made a normal taxi and takeoff. The flying fortress began a smooth climb, but then suddenly stalled due to its high nose-up attitude. The aircraft rolled on one wing, fell from the sky, and burst into flames upon impact.

Putt, Benton, and Igo—although seriously burned—were able to stagger out of the wreckage to the arriving safety crews. Hill and Tower were trapped in the wreckage but were rescued. Both men later died of their injuries.

The Model 299 was substantially more complex than previous aircraft. The new plane required the pilot to manage the four engines, retractable landing gear, newly designed wing flaps, electric trim tabs that needed adjustment to maintain control at different airspeeds, and constant speed propellers whose pitch had to be regulated with hydraulic controls, among many other features.

The investigation found "pilot error" as the cause. Hill, unfamiliar with the aircraft, had neglected to release the elevator lock prior to takeoff. Once airborne, Tower, Boeing's chief test pilot, realized what was happening and tried to reach the lock handle, but it was too late, his fate was sealed.

It appeared that the Model 299 was dead. Some newspapers had dubbed it as "too much plane for one man to fly." Most of the aircraft contracts went to the runner-up, the Douglas DB-1. The Air Corps brass gave Boeing a chance to keep the Model 299 project alive. Twelve aircraft were ordered for further testing.

The pilots of the Model 299, renamed the B-17 Flying Fortress, sat down and put their heads together (this was also a historic event as pilots had never before put their heads together for a productive reason—it was also the last time that this occurrence was ever recorded). They needed a way to ensure that everything that was required to operate the aircraft effectively was actually done and that nothing was forgotten.

What resulted was a pilot's checklist. The checklist had four parts: takeoff, flight, before landing, and after landing. The B-17 proved that it was not "too much airplane for one man to fly," after all. It was simply too complex for any one man to remember all the steps in the proper order. These groundbreaking checklists added a significant safety margin and standardization to the aviation community globally.

The US Army accepted the B-17, and eventually ordered 12,731 of the heavy bombers. With the use of simple checklists, the complex flying behemoth was now able to operate safely and went on to conduct the devastating bombing campaign of the Air Corps across Nazi Germany and other occupied territories.

Abbreviated and Expanded Checklists

The B-17s were the first airframe to use a checklist, but they certainly were not the last.

In the C-130, we use checklists every single flight, and I can't even begin to imagine operating an aircraft like the Herk without the checklists. We have what's called the abbreviated checklist, which is about thirty pages long and what we carry in our hands. It has all of the items to check. Then there is what's called the expanded checklist. The expanded checklist is the one that delves deeper into each checklist item. For example, the abbreviated checklist states "Hydraulic Panel: Set," but the expanded checklist states exactly how this checklist item will be performed and how to make the hydraulic panel actually set.

There are two general ways to use a checklist. The flow method is the fastest and the one that is generally the technique used by airline-type pilots. In the flow method the pilot will go through a flow, from left to right or top to bottom, and hit all the items and flip all the switches to where they need to be, using their memory. Then they pick up their abbreviated checklist and go step-by-step to verify that they did indeed check every single item. This is a very common way of running a checklist.

There's also the step-by-step. This one's a little more common with pilots who are new to the aircraft. The step-by-step technique is when the pilot will actually pick up the checklist, read one item, and then switch the switch.

This is also what is done with the challenge-response type in which one individual reads off the item while the other aviator responds with the correct response after having executed the action. A simple example goes like this: "Altimeters" is called out by the copilot, and "Set two nine nine two" is the response of the pilot. It's a much slower way of doing it, but it's by no means wrong and in some situations absolutely correct. The challenge response is how the crews of the C-130 operate.

Real Estate Checklists

I am not ashamed to personally admit that when I assemble Ikea furniture I follow the instructions (checklist) because I have more than once put furniture together backward and then had to redouble my efforts and quadruple my frustration to assemble it correctly.

Now how does that work for real estate?

When developing checklists, we use the flow method. An abbreviated checklist tells us at a higher level everything that needs to be checked. For example, under due diligence, we check crime reports, physical conditions, submarket, and demographics among others. In this abbreviated checklist of demographics, the checklist just says "Demographics."

We go much deeper in detail on the demographics in the expanded checklist. Were the demographics checked? Yes. So if the demographics box is checked, what is the story behind its completion? The check means that the expanded checklist was also completed.

The expanded checklist has ethnic information on the people living in the area, the median household income within one and three miles, crime rates, locations of sex offenders, population growth projections and actual growth, education levels, traffic counts, how far locals commute to work, if they work from home, if they work and play nearby, and all sorts of other pertinent information that gives the highest resolution picture of the people in the area and potential tenants in the submarket. Everything that can possibly be learned about the people who live within the one-mile and three-mile submarket is the information of interest.

Checking demographics seems easy enough. In this step if it is discovered that everybody living within a community is working at the Ford factory, for example, that fact will leave the target property or market with a lot of risk. If the factory shuts down with no replacement, a new Detroit wasteland could be made overnight. This is just one of the factors to consider in developing a checklist of your own.

"Utilities." Check. There is a much deeper explanation of the utilities as well on the expanded checklist. Just some of the answers that must be uncovered stem from the questions regarding how much the tenants are paying for power, trash, water, and gas. Are the tenants paying for water or is it master metered and a cost that the owner pays? How much is the owner paying for power, water, gas, telephone, internet, and other expenses that are variable?

Knowing this information will open up opportunities for cash savings in utilities. These types of audits are simple to perform and are easy to overlook during the euphoria of buying a new, sexy property. If the water bill is higher than what is known to be the going rate, for example, open the expanded checklist to find a source of the issue and don't give the current owner any credit because they often have no idea what is happening at their own property. There may be a leak in the water pipes underground; the pool may have a leak and the pool needs more water every other day; there could be double billing, toilets constantly running.

The rabbit hole goes deeper and deeper into the individual items than just the abbreviated checklist. Yes, many of these items are time consuming, but it is also wildly profitable because knowing a property inside and out can be priceless.

The abbreviated checklist itself may be only a page, but when combined with the expanded checklist for, say, due diligence, it could be ten to twenty pages long, and to gather all the information to make a complete checklist takes time and focus.

Eventually, there will be enough comfort to get into the flow method of the checklist, but starting in the step-by-step method is the best way to build a checklist of your own. There will come a point when the checklist is so ingrained in the process that it is second nature and there will be no reason not to use them.

Checklists save time, money, and energy, because nothing is forgotten and nothing is overlooked. Before I had a checklist, I would skip items I thought were not important or that didn't seem as if they would turn into big deals. I soon learned something about myself; I can handle bad news, I just don't like surprises, and I really don't like surprises on property that I own.

If we discover the bad news about a foundation crack before buying a property, that is really good information to have. If we discover the unfortunate and expensive fix after purchasing a property, all we can do is kick ourselves for not having run through all of the checklists—because foundations are on the inspection checklist.

Checklist.

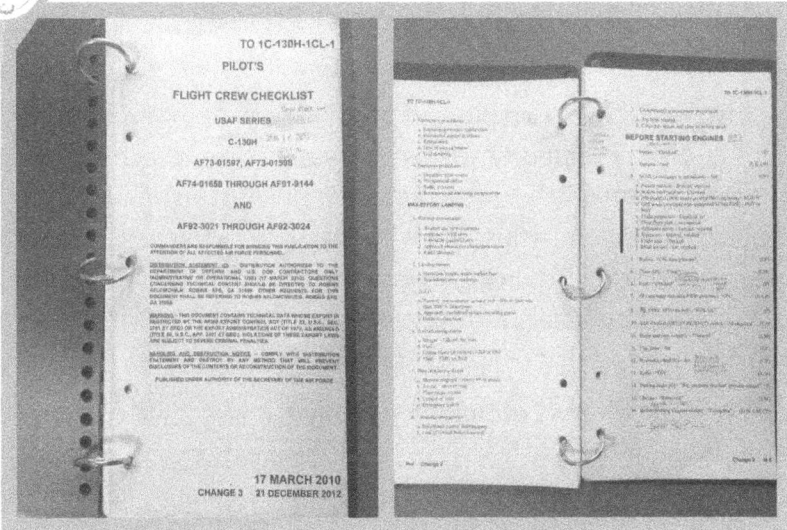

Operations Manual and More

When the individual checklists are created, they are then added to the operations manual. The OM is a living document that is constantly being improved upon. If there is ever a question that the OM can't answer, we find a logical and best-practices answer and then update the OM.

Every new person who comes to work for me and my team gets to read the OM the same way as new pilots to the Middle East read the SPINs—the new employee can expect the fire hose effect so that they can get up to speed right away. Even if the new employee can't complete all the tasks right away, they will at least have the awareness that a policy and procedure is in place and where to find the information.

I personally use checklists daily. I don't have the step-by-step checklist out during my day-to-day but certainly the flow checklist. One of the things that I have recently started doing—and I got the idea from Jordon Belfort, the Wolf of Wall

Street—is to put my six-month goals/plans on the wallpaper on my phone in order of importance. I have an iPhone, so on the lock or home screen, before I can even get to the apps, I have a picture of my to-do checklist.

Instead of having a picture of my dog, my wife, or my airplane (not in order of importance, by the way), I have a picture of all the things I am going to accomplish in the next six months. It is a boring black-and-white list with no more than six items. For example, writing this book was the number two item on the list until I completed it. Selling one of the properties I own was the fourth item and that property sold just the other day.

Every day dozens of times a day, my list is right there in my face. The number one item is to purchase another great property that fits into our business plan and model. That one's still in the works, but I think about it every day because that goal checklist is right in front of me.

The End of Maverick

Tom Wolfe's book *The Right Stuff* tells the story of our first astronauts and charts the demise of maverick Chuck Yeager's test-pilot culture of the 1950s. It was a culture defined by how unbelievably dangerous the job was. Test pilots strapped themselves into machines and could barely control the power and complexity, and a quarter of them were killed on the job. The pilots had to have focus, daring, wits, and an ability to improvise—the right stuff.

But as knowledge of how to control the risks of flying accumulated—as checklists and flight simulators became more prevalent and sophisticated—the danger diminished, values of safety and conscientiousness prevailed, and the rock-star status of the test pilots was gone.

A checklist is only as good as the discipline to follow it and all the substeps—much like a seatbelt is no good to the driver if it isn't buckled. If a checklist fails to address an issue or addresses it incorrectly or the steps could be done better, change it, update it, and remember it is a living document, and there are no right answers, but there sure are wrong ones. Then communicate with the rest of your team about the change and have them adopt the new checklist.

I'm sure these real estate checklists won't save anyone's life, but they will definitely advance business objectives and will help clients, investors, and everyone else who is working with me. Most importantly I can sleep at night knowing I didn't miss any steps because sometimes the airplane really is too much for one man to fly.

THE DEVIL IS
THE DETAILS

Never neglect details. When everyone's mind is dulled or
distracted, the leader must be doubly vigilant.
—General Colin Powell

et out of the way, Joe!" the pilot shouted into his headset as
the roar of two of the four propeller-driven engines spun.
The 120,000-pound aircraft started to move forward on
the tarmac in a gradual but noticeable left-hand turn. The pilot
desperate to stop the aircraft, threw the throttles in reverse and
stood on the brakes—anything to get the out-of-control plane
to stop.

As the copilot, I looked in the vicinity of my left knee to
check the hydraulic pressures on the lower control panel, and I
flipped a switch up. Immediately the aircraft came to an abrupt
and violent stop from its unauthorized movement. The pilot
returned the throttles to idle, and we all looked at each other
with mouths agape and eyes wide in utter disbelief of how
quickly the very normal procedure of starting the engines could
have become a near-fatal incident.

The early morning sun witnessed the event in Yuma, Arizona, situated just minutes away from the Mexican border. Without a cloud in the sky, the sun was much hotter than what would have been expected by a Midwesterner like myself.

The crew and I were on a weeklong trip to the Military Free-Fall School. Our mission: to take twenty or so instructors and brand new special operations (special forces) students to 13,000 feet and let them jump out of the back of our C-130 Hercules to perform High Altitude Low Opening (HALO) or High Altitude High Opening (HAHO) jumps and then return with the empty aircraft to pick up twenty or so more jumpers and do it all over again. We would do this about a dozen times a day for four days—fatigue and complacency were an inevitable occurrence. Simply, it just gets boring.

How could a fully qualified and proficient crew allow a plane to run away? And how did this movement happen anyway? What lessons, while embarrassing, could be learned from this mistake?

How it happened was simple. It is simple to explain, and simple to remediate, but just below the surface of this event were a couple of troubling mistakes.

The problem of the runaway plane was caused by me not having put a tiny switch in the right position—in this case, the emergency position. The switch provides hydraulic pressure to the parking brake, which holds the aircraft still while we start the engines. After the second engine on the right side was started, enough power was produced to move the parked airplane with asymmetrical thrust forward and to the left.

But wait, you ask! Isn't there a checklist for this? Aren't you preaching the use of checklists? Aren't you pilot-types always double-checking each other's work?

And the answer is yes we do. I won't make excuses for myself or for the crew; we messed up. We were tired and we were complacent, we wanted the trip to be over. While I could go into all of the details of what happened, know this: three individuals were *required* to check the hydraulic pressures and the parking brake before engine start, per the checklist. Well we didn't or we did and didn't catch it. Consequently, someone else could have paid the ultimate price for our inaction and inattention.

It Is Your Responsibility

Small and critically important items like this happen in real estate firms every day. The smallest error in underwriting calculations or letting an undesirable tenant slip through the cracks can have massive and long-lasting repercussions. Real estate companies must do everything in their power to avoid the pitfalls of these, on the surface, seemingly minor issues.

A great technique to deal with details is to create tailored checklists (the subject of the previous story, for those who are skipping around in this book), developing operations manuals for all levels of the company, and then having rigorous quality assurance oversight to prevent any lapses in protocol. Some people may call this red tape or unnecessary or even overkill. I call it good business practices.

Have checklists that are integrated in operating procedures that address every issue that has been experienced, or you have imagined experiencing (see the story on chair flying for the Air Force version of visualization). If an unusual occurrence would happen, even if the likelihood of it happening again is small, put it in the operating manual, then communicate with everyone what was learned. This type of recording, foresight, communication, and system building is central to top-notch performance in the field—any field, including an airfield.

While we aren't perfect we certainly strive for perfection.

I hear all the time from self-proclaimed business experts to keep the big picture in mind, and let someone else deal with the details. No way. All I can do is shake my head because the devil isn't in the details—the devil *is* the details! With a big-picture mindset, so many important and sometimes very small items could easily be overlooked or flat out ignored.

Big Problems Start Out as Fixable Small Problems

I often see apartments not having proper drainage from the downspouts. More often than not, and take a look for yourself at various properties, the downspouts from the gutters (which are probably clogged with five years' worth of leaves, pine needles, and squirrel carcasses) dump large amounts of water at the foot of the building.

This is normally not an issue for the first seven years or so, but somewhere around eight to ten years, this large amount of water will slowly and surely disrupt the foundation of the building. Why? Well buildings are built on dirt, and with all of that water drip, drip, dripping for such a long period of time, the dirt becomes mud. Mud is soft and it moves, especially when there is something heavy on it like a forty-unit apartment building—the foundation that was not designed to move starts to crack or make the building slant in what can sometimes be a visible angle. Thankfully the technology now exists to correct this issue and square up the building—all that is needed is six-figures-plus to make it stand right again.

In this case something as simple as adding ten-foot downspout extensions to get the water well away from the foundation will prevent these massive and expensive foundation problems. The cost of this preemptive action: eight dollars, ten if the fancy downspouts are installed.

I'll buy a property that has these drainage and foundation issues. The only challenge is that I am not going to pay for it, the seller will. And I am sure that if they only knew that $200 worth of downspout extensions could have saved them $100,000 or more at the closing table, they would have gone out to the property and screwed them on themselves. Maybe the owners read a book that told them the management company or asset manager would have caught the problem—because isn't that just a little, insignificant detail?

Attention to Detail

The loss of the attention to detail happens either acutely or insidiously. The immediate loss of attention to the small things happens for any number of reasons. A larger, more important issue or event may have arisen (for example, a property fire or a new property opening down the street threatens to take tenants away), and the small items such as downspouts don't seem as important or there are not enough brain bytes or people to attend to the little things that need attention.

Sometimes this is for the best. Obviously, if an event requires immediate attention, then by all means move resources to take advantage of the opportunity or negate the losses caused by a negative event. The good news about the quick change of attention is that generally it is easy to get back in the grove to attend to the smaller details.

Insidious loss of the granular attention to detail is the most dangerous, because it is often not noticed (the cracked entry steps, the broken door hinge, the frayed carpet) or if it is realized, no one does anything about it ("Not my job."). This is often because people become lazy with their property and don't take the action needed to ensure the details are nurtured.

The challenge may arise because a firm is getting larger and isn't hiring or outsourcing the people it needs to back-fill the jobs that a more senior executive or founder once held. This is a common growing pain in all businesses and one that all growing businesses will always have unless a plan is in place to address it on a continuing basis.

This slow loss of attention to detail has the potential to become the biggest threat to a company or property. The small things (the tears in the screens, the chipping paint, and burned out lightbulbs) may never get the attention that they require because they are simply abandoned. No one ever thinks or takes action to remediate these problems ever again—they are orphaned.

These small details then start to fester and become larger and larger problems in the future. Prospective tenants see that a property is not being taken care of and look to other places that have a strong pride of ownership. The worst part is that they will never tell you that they think your property is dumpy because they will never return your calls or emails. If these small problems are fundamental in scope to the business, they could eventually lead to the demise of the whole company or cause a whole lot of embarrassment, loss of revenue, increase in expenses, and loss of trust from the clients.

Check and Then Double-Check

One of the positives about making mistakes such as not flipping that switch on the C-130 is that I will carry it with me for a lifetime. How many times do you think I check that switch when we are starting engines? I'll give you a hint: at least twice.

Looking back, while it was a tough lesson to learn, it is one that I will never forget, and the best part is that I have the opportunity to tell others that while the detail may be small, it could have had some devilish consequences.

STAY IN POSITION

Quitting is the easiest thing to do.
—Robert Kiyosaki

I could feel my heartbeat in the tips of my fingers as I had a death grip on the stick.

"Now just slide into position…take a little more lead," my instructor in the backseat said. "Power back a hair…and… PERFECT! You are in perfect position, call in," he shouted with a mix of pride and a healthy dose of urgency.

"Two's in," I squeaked on the radio as my 1,100-shaft horsepower T-6 Texan II was a very close ten feet behind and below another T-6 flown by a fellow student pilot. Calling "in position" gave the other student permission to begin a series of flight maneuvers that taught us how to fly in close—fingertip close—formation, which is required learning for all military pilots. It was my job, my duty, my entire reason for life to stay in position, even when it was incredibly unnatural and unbelievably uncomfortable.

The bubble canopy was of no help on that scorching September day in West Texas. I felt like I was an ant under a magnifying glass of heat from the thermal hate of the southwestern sun. This was the least of my worries. I felt the harness from my ejection seat dig into my shoulders as the formation rolled into our aggressive maneuvers.

Fundamentals of Formation Flight

When air-to-air combat started in World War I, it was every man for himself. Teamwork was not part of the modus operandi. Air-to-air combat engagements are also known as dogfights. These dogfights were so chaotic they were called fur balls because of the completely unorganized, three-dimensional mess that was created by an uncountable number of machine-gun–armed biplanes in a small corner of the European sky.

By the Second World War, fighter pilots found that it was safer to work in pairs. Ever since this revelation, military pilots and more specifically fighter pilots have gone to combat working together.

The reason for this pairing in combat is simple: a pilot cannot see what is directly behind him. No matter how much he turns his head, there will always be a blind spot even with the use of mirrors. When two aircraft fly in formation, the leader and his wingman can visually clear the other's rear position for hostile fighters. They call it "checking your six" (if twelve o'clock is straight ahead, then six is behind you). A lone airplane is forever vulnerable from a rear attack.

The most effective use of an airplane as a weapon of war both defensively and offensively is when it acts as teams of a single unit. Consequently, learning how to fly in formation is a must for all military pilots, even pilots who will not be engaging in dogfights. The C-130 makes extensive use of formation flying for primarily one reason and that is to put more troops, weapons, and equipment in a small area all at the same time. There is a multiplying effect when C-130s work together. If airdropping two Humvees is good, then airdropping four Humvees is even better.

The smallest unit in a formation of planes is two aircraft called an element. The element leader also known as the flight leader is primarily responsible for the conduct of the element, its safe navigation, and mission accomplishment. The job of the wingman or non-element leader is to maintain proper position in relation to the flight leader and support him in any way required.

Back to Business

"Get back in position!" the instructor snapped. I had slowly drifted out of position—not much but enough to be noticed by the demanding instructor.

Maybe I moved away slightly because I was not able to fight my natural urge to get farther away from another airplane flying

Two Laughlin Air Force Base T-6 Texan IIs in close formation.

230 miles per hour, or perhaps I didn't have the guts for this precision flying. Either way, nobody cared, not my instructor, not my fellow student, and not even me. All I knew, all I believed, and the entire essence of my being was to get back in position in spite of the long list of excuses I could come up with to move farther away from flight lead.

There is nothing that will clear your mind better than the fight to stay in position.

The Position of Real Estate

Years later I was faced with the same challenge of staying in position on a real estate transaction. Deal fatigue had begun to set in. Deal fatigue occurs when a deal drags on and on and the partnership faces one obstruction after another that makes it seem as if the deal may never get closed.

In this case my eye started to wander to the exit—I was going to peel out of the proverbial formation for ego-preservation reasons and because I wanted to just quit. I started to come up with numerous excuses to end the deal to save face, but what really happened is that I just wanted to not deal with the enormous amount of discomfort that I was experiencing. I wanted out even though I knew that I must stick in there and stay in position.

I am sure that had I quit, I would have come up with some wonderful and reasonable excuse. I would have created an excuse that others would have certainly understood, and if I had invented a good enough excuse, I may have even started to believe in my own lie, which would have given me the evidence that I needed to feel better about my inability to close the deal.

In this specific case, I was unable to secure the debt that was required to buy my targeted property. I went to one bank after another with the same result; I was strung along for a bit before they ultimately rejected me for one Mickey Mouse reason or another. I started to feel like this deal would never get closed, and I began to lose faith in both the property and myself. Even though I knew this property would be a huge success and take my firm to the next level—I just wanted to quit and then later feel sorry for myself.

As I would lie awake at night thinking about my earnest money that was about to be lost to the seller for not being able to close on the property after the contingencies had been lifted, the unforgettable words "stay in position" came to my mind. Then and there I resolved to stay in position regardless of the personal cost to myself. It was my duty to myself and my investors to perform in the sterling manner in which I told them I would and to protect their investment, regardless of how uncomfortable or unnatural it was for me—just like that day in the scorching air above West Texas within fingertips of another plane screaming across the sky.

A month or so after my resolve was steeled, the property closed. The property has gone on to be a huge success and was a real launch pad for future acquisitions and investor relations. The property has followed the management and improvement plan to the letter and has surpassed even my admittedly lofty expectations.

Staying in position is not a place, it is a pursuit. Everyone can get in position, sooner or later. But staying in position is the hard part. And here is the secret: you aren't perfect, the plan isn't perfect, but when you find yourself out of position or falling out of position, you better do your damnedest to get back to where you should be because it is more than just you who would be let down if you aren't—even if you convince yourself otherwise.

Tenacity and Patience

Successful people attribute many characteristics to their success; and numerous articles, books, and interviews delve into the lives of successful people—so it would be redundant to rehash them in this book. But I would like to explore the two traits that are explicitly related to formation flying and the traits that I have myself spent a lot of focused and deliberate time to develop: tenacity and patience.

Tenacity by definition is the quality or fact of being very persistent. To have resolve, to push forward in light of bad news or unfavorable events, and having the wherewithal to just keep climbing and reaching one's goal or objectives.

The story I shared about my unwillingness to quit when I was learning to fly formation is a perfect example of when I had to put on my big boy pants and dig deep to find my inner tenacity and push forward. In spite of the overwhelming desire to quit to be both physically safe and safe from the possibility and shame of failure, I knew I had to push forward—it was just one of those crossroads moments in life.

To this day I am always honing my tenacity. When most people learn of the projects I am engaged in simultaneously, they tell me that I am doing too much. That I need to slow down and get some balance in my life. They tell me that I should take more time off or instead of reading business books that I should read for pleasure. They tell me that writing this book is silly and I should instead go to the pool with them and drink beer.

But some people never criticize my tenacity or my projects. They simply nod their heads when they hear about my master plan and give me small critiques or new ideas on how I can reach my goals. They give me these pieces of advice while we sit in their high-end suite waiting for the concert to start. You see, the people who have mastered their own tenacity and have a clear picture of the future are very successful themselves.

When I once asked for business advice from a man who is beyond wealthy from the formation and growth of his own companies, he told me, "You can easily be more successful than I am. All you have to do is work eighty hours a week for twenty years. But don't worry, you will get there." Now that is tenacious!

Some people—not many—are huge action takers. Action takers are people who make things happen. They're the movers and shakers of our society, and they move the earth forward. I am always in awe of their capabilities, their vision, and their ability to get things done. But sometimes they need to put their action engine in idle. I most certainly am not criticizing them for taking action on any level—but sometimes the bigger picture doesn't seem to be in focus.

Imagine that business is akin to a large, complicated game of chess. There are a number of basics to be learned before the game can even be played. Once the basics have been mastered and the rules fully understood, the game really starts to get interesting. The challenge is that moving pieces all over the board by taking action may feel good—it may feel that forward action is being made. However, progress is normally not being made. What is really happening is that the pieces of the business are just being rearranged in a haphazard manner with no thought to the future or how to leverage the pieces of the business for future opportunities.

It is my firm belief that it is far more important to fully develop a plan for the future to make the plan a reality than just taking a lot of action with no real guidance or purpose. An example of my point is this book. Let me explain.

I currently believe that the real estate market as a whole is in what I call a high plateau. What this means is that all indications show that transactional volume (buying and selling) are at a feverish pace.

A case in point is that I just sold a property in twenty-one days—lightning fast. That is from the time the marketing package was released to the actual closing of the property—the cash in my pocket day was three weeks later. The buyer paid all cash, with no contingencies or inspections and never even saw the property! If these are the people that I am competing against to buy properties in my niche, there is no competition because I can't and won't compete against this kind of buyer.

The market is also in a high plateau because the vacancies are steady at historic lows, rents are at historic highs, and sales prices are steady as well, neither increasing nor decreasing.

Although I understand that not all markets are the same, and of course there are hidden deals in every town, the properties that I want are just getting fewer and further between. The inability to find properties that meet my criteria that I set forth to my investors has caused me to switch the focus of my intensity of action from finding, negotiating, and buying property to writing this book, starting a full-service property management company, and working on better communicating with the people and companies that I work with now and want to work with into the future.

This book from inception to creation took less than three months. This book was created to start a relationship with you, the reader, and to give you insights into how I have successfully taken my military experience and created a long-term–focused real estate firm. Perhaps you can meet similar goals too.

If I had kept my level of action trying to buy properties that are a good fit for Sierra Whiskey, all that would happen is that I would become stressed out and I would start to get very frustrated—both are negative mental spaces. So I spent time to move my other chess pieces around on the board to be in an excellent position to strike when opportunity does arise again. And since I took the time to position my firm better, we will be able to make an even bigger impact when the winds of the market change in our favor again.

This all comes down to patience and not becoming a motivated buyer. Motivated buyers generally make bad decisions on the properties that they buy—such as the property purchased is not structured well for the owners and investors to have the largest possibility of success.

Have the discipline and the fortitude to tell your investors that "we have to wait for our pitch"—because we don't have to buy anything and we would much rather have no property than a property we wish we didn't have. Have the tenacity to push forward and the patience to know how and when to get back into position.

By the time I became proficient at flying in a tight precision formation, the Air Force graduated me to the next phase of training, and I never flew fingertip formation again. While I do fly formation regularly in the Herk, we fly at a much larger spacing that doesn't require much of the intense—feel it in your fingertips—concentration. I really learned to enjoy that type of close flying, when I was able to relax, focus, be patient, and then tenaciously get back into position.

GARBAGE IN, GARBAGE OUT

A wise person is hungry for knowledge,
while the fool feeds on trash.
—Proverbs 15:14

"One thousand above." The student clearly and calmly stated into the headset microphone.

"Five hundred above." In an uninterested and almost toneless voice, the aviator called out to the crew.

This was the voice of a second lieutenant and a soon-to-be navigator in the United States Air Force. The student was near the end of his navigator training that would prepare him to be able to globally navigate a jet aircraft in nearly any weather condition. It was the fall of 2006.

The numbers that were being called out were the number of feet above the landing runway; the callout was required per regulations. It was clear that the student had chair flown this mission already and was ready for it to be over with. He had been sitting in what felt like a dimly lit meat locker for the better part of four hours.

"Three hundred above." A smooth if not agitated voice sang. He was getting this number from the barometric altimeter. Aircrews get the current pressure from the airfield weather station, and then the aviators manually set the barometric altimeters into the instrument.

But wait! This isn't making sense. The altimeter says that the aircraft is 300 feet off the ground, but the navigation radar is turning very black—an indication that the radar waves are hitting something big and aren't penetrating through the mass. His mind races as to what the issue could be. He settles on the idea of a failure of the radar because his altimeter is showing that he is above the terrain.

The radar altimeter, which shoots radar waves directly beneath the aircraft and then those waves bounce off the surface and register on the radar altimeter how high the aircraft is actually off the ground, is decreasing at an alarming rate and heading to zero.

"GO AROUND!" he shouted trying to stand out of his seat, held in place only by his seat belt. As the pilot executed his go-around maneuver, it was too late. The aircraft impacted the side of the mountain at 150 miles per hour.

There would be no survivors.

The Reality of the Situation

Had this scenario been in a real airplane, I would be dead.

Fortunately, I was in a simulator. The simulator is a place where students can learn to do tasks that are either too dangerous to perform for real in the airplane or can be done in a much more cost-effective manner in what is also known as the "box"—a big computer game.

I was twenty-two years old, and there were no actual casualties other than my ego. However, the learning event was 100 percent avoidable and completely my fault.

You see in this iteration in the simulator, we were landing in the mountainous country of Japan. The barometric altimeter requires inches of mercury to be set rather than using hectopascals, because there is no way to directly input the metric system. The error was in my translation of the barometric pressure reported to me in the metric hectopascals as opposed to the imperial inches of mercury.

As the navigator it was my responsibility to look up the conversion in a reference book and then pass the imperial setting to the rest of the crew so that they may all set their altimeters correctly.

The challenge here was while I was bored in the last few minutes of the simulator ride, the previous four hours or so, I was so completely task saturated that I felt as if I was hanging on to the back of the airplane rather than taking control of the situation and shaping the flight in the manner that was within regulations to complete the mission at hand. I had let down my guard at the end and paid the ultimate price—sort of.

"This is a classic case of garbage in, garbage out," my instructor debriefed me. Wait, what? What does that even mean?

"The garbage in, garbage out idiom has its history in the computer science field and has the broad stroke of meaning that the end result is adversely affected by earlier direct inputs," he explained.

Another way of conceptualizing garbage in, garbage out is that the quality of the output is directly affected by the input. This saying would be very true for a high-performance athlete who has a poor diet. The athlete will never be able to have a great performance with a poor diet. Garbage in, garbage out.

In my incident the issue was that I put garbage in the altimeter, a wrong altimeter setting, and I got garbage out with an incorrect altitude that eventually caused a crash.

In the real estate world, I also use simulators. When preparing to purchase a property, I use sophisticated software to underwrite the property, the income and the expenses, and the market as a whole. While the calculations are complicated, the program itself is rather dumb. It does exactly what I input, will execute its work with no questions asked, and will never catch any mistakes.

In commercial real estate I have heard stories of projects, properties, and partnerships going bust because they put out a garbage product. Of course the product was garbage! Look at all the junk they put into it: poor debt structure, equity capital stack that never made sense, or market projections that were well off base and never materialized. Garbage in, garbage out.

More to the point, it reminds me of property that I was preparing to buy a few years ago. I was desperate to find a loan for a property that was undervalued and was going to do very well after my firm purchased it. The issue was that I was not as prepared to speak with the lenders when I approached them, and the time line to closing was short.

Many just turned me down flat when I spoke with them. However, I did find one company that was willing to make the loan happen. Things were going well in the underwriting phase, and then inexplicably I was told that the "markets had changed" and that the terms of the loan would be drastically different from what was originally quoted. I chalked this up to the unethical practice of bait-and-switch; they must have sensed my need to make the loan happen in such a short time frame and were testing to see if I was the sucker born in that minute.

Had I accepted this debt structure, the property would have been in seriously bad shape within six months. There was no way that the property could have paid for the debt. Sometimes this is called "loan-to-own," which means that the lender gives onerous terms that they know the borrower won't be able to handle in hopes that they will be able to foreclose on the property, wipe out the investor's equity, and get back a good property for a steal—literally.

I told them that they could go fly a kite and to lose my number. This is a perfect example of garbage in, garbage out. The garbage would have been so vile that the partnership would have gotten just as horrible results out.

Taking Care of Your System

Avoid at all costs putting garbage in the system especially when purchasing a property. Make sure that there is a solid collection of all of the most up-to-date information from various sources. Use sources that contradict each other, and then make decisions based on the good, the bad, and the ugly, not just on the information that would make the project look the best. Accuracy is important.

Often overestimating the costs and time to complete a project and underestimating the income and favorable market conditions with the knowledge of how easy it is for things to go sideways due to forces beyond anyone's control can be a great tactic. Fixing problems at the property may take a little more time, and money, but these factors have already been accounted for because there was never any garbage in the system to start with.

When there is no garbage in the system, performance will be at peak levels. In business, performance has a very easy unit of measurement: dollars. First, has the capital been protected that has been entrusted with the firm? The answer is always yes because investor and bank money is treated better than any other money. Okay, now that the investors' and bank's money is safe, are all of the available resources being used in a cost-effective and reasonable manner? Once again the answer is yes. Make sure that funds are not being spent on unnecessary or frivolous expenditures.

Look daily for garbage in the system and remove it with great prejudice when it is found—this is a defensive tactic, but often the best offense is a great defense. Once it is known that everything has been done to safeguard funds by removing garbage, then profits will really start to roll in.

When I am reviewing my systems and checking for garbage, I am often reminded of the time I flew the plane into the side of a mountain in Japan. The experience has served me well, and I am glad I can share it here now. I know how well the saying of garbage in, garbage out works because I have never again crashed either in the aircraft or on a real estate deal. Since the garbage is gone, my new mantra is quality in, quality out.

My First Foray into the Mountain

After having graduated from navigator school, I became an Electronic Warfare Officer (EWO) on the top-secret spy plane the RC-135 Rivet Joint, stationed in Omaha at Offutt Air Force Base, where the underground and overhead nuclear deterrent force was stationed. Offutt was actually the first place Air Force One with President George Bush on board went during the world-changing day of September 11, 2001.

Not one to put all my eggs in one basket, I took a step into the world of real estate. I had been working with a gentleman who was showing me how to use a strategy called wholesaling houses and also learning how to buy mobile homes. The wholesaling was pretty much a bust as it required an extensive rolodex of buyers and sellers of houses that are in need of rehab. It also required a frothy market of transactions, which at the time was as cold as the Nebraska winter in 2009. Now mobile homes, this was something that I could sink my teeth into.

The mobile home niche was quite brilliant in its simplicity. The idea is that there are thousands of mobile home dwellers in any given city, and Omaha was no exception. The market was created because the people who would buy and live in a mobile home are generally of limited means and are unable to buy a used mobile home from a resident/seller simply because they don't have the cash on hand to do so. Now they could go out and get a loan, but lenders generally don't want to lend on $10,000 worth of what is technically personal property that has wheels so it might not be there three weeks from the sale.

I would buy the mobile home directly from the person who lived in it—I'd pay in $100 bills if they would give me a discount (which they all did). The seller was generally desperate to sell because there wasn't much of a market for people who could buy the home—once again because of the limited cash of the buyer, and the seller may have any number of issues with former lovers, the law, or maybe a new job out of town (I heard it all).

After buying the property for cash, I would put money into the home to make it attractive to the type of buyer that I wanted, and then I would sell the mobile home on terms also known as rent-to-own.

I paid the guy for the first mobile home that I bought with fifteen $100 bills counted out on the hood of his truck, as we signed a sales agreement and the title. Then his old yellow lab barely made the jump into the cab of that beat-up blue truck, and he drove off—I never saw or heard from him again. That night was the beginning of the hardest winter in Omaha in twenty-five years, and the pipes froze and burst. The good news was that it was so cold that the leaking water quickly froze, so the mess was minimal and the water bill was also low (a simple checklist could have prevented this).

The market for rent-to-own properties was immensely strong. I would simply market the property with a sign in the yard and a craigslist ad. The property would be sold on my program in less than a week. The buyer would sign a promissory note along with some other important looking paperwork and, pending a background check, would get to move in.

I didn't do credit checks because all of their credit was trash, mainly because of medical bills or a foreclosed house just a few years prior. I didn't really care; I was much more interested in criminal background and current employment. Last thing I wanted to deal with was a violent felon or someone who couldn't pay me.

The buyer would then put down $500 to $1,000 and would agree to an easy monthly payment for five years. I did seven of these deals and not one of them asked what the interest rate was or what the total cost of the purchase was, even though they were disclosed in the paperwork. The answer would have been about 12 percent interest and a lot more than sticker price.

Before you start getting upset with me taking advantage of these people, please understand that they simply didn't care! They only cared that they got a nice, clean mobile home in a safe park for $250 a month.

One of the most exciting aspects about having started with mobile homes is that the same tactics and techniques used for the $1,500 mobile homes are used with properties ten and one hundred times as valuable. All of the following steps are used in mobile homes as with high-end apartments: finding the niche, understanding the customer, understanding the market, marketing and advertising, finding a property to purchase, negotiating the property's sale, finding appropriate debt (if used), ensuring the proper paperwork is in order, managing the tenants and the property, and of course selling the property with a good exit strategy when the time comes.

Now the time line on a mobile home purchase could be as short as a few days while the apartment complex could take months, but when both are boiled down to their raw elements, they may seem different. But ultimately they have the same aspects, and the same responsibility is required for both. Looking back, I am glad and even proud to have gotten my real estate start in this niche, which prepared me well for what lay ahead on my path.

A Bridge Too Far

I ran this mobile home business for a few years and ended up being able to buy and sell a handful of homes when I was selected to go to Air Force pilot training by the Missouri Air National Guard in the fall of 2009. I separated from full-time military service and the healthy paycheck that came with it. The challenge with accepting the new dream job other than the loss of the income was that I would have to wait eighteen months before I would actually report to the pilot training base.

To supplement my income, I was sure that I would be able to graduate to the next level of real estate investments and be able to flip at least a few houses while I waited more than a year and a half to go to pilot training and get a full-time paycheck again. While the mobile home income was coming in, it would not be able to support even the most modest lifestyle. My timing couldn't have been worse, it was just after the global economic meltdown, and with no money, income, experience, or connections, I was a poor choice for any lender. Without the cash flow coming from Uncle Sam, I slowly depleted my savings, and I cashed out my 401(k) in a desperate attempt for funds. I got a temporary job as a census enumerator to make ends meet, but when that gig ended, so did my time in Omaha.

I had to take the nuclear option: move back in with my parents (and to round off the cliché, I would move into their basement in the same room where I spent my teenage years). So I packed up what I had and moved back to the St. Louis area. At least I had a dog to come with me.

I spent most of those eighteen months working out, studying real estate and finance, and trying to buy a house to flip with the same poor results as in Nebraska. It was spring of 2011 (which in hindsight turned out to be the bottom of the national real estate market and would have been the perfect time to buy anything made of sticks and bricks).

In the summer of 2011 through sheer patience and waking up every morning, I finally made it to Del Rio, Texas, home of Laughlin Air Force Base where I learned how not to fly into a mountain—and finally realized my lifelong dream of becoming an Air Force pilot—a trek eleven years in the making.

CHAIR FLYING

Hold a picture of yourself long and steadily
enough in your mind's eye,
and you will be drawn toward it.
—Napoleon Hill

Normally, cringes of anticipation and apathy are a common sight if there is any mention of chair flying to any aviator, myself included. To any new aviator or any aviator flying a new-to-them airplane or in an unfamiliar environment or situation, they will know exactly what chair flying means.

For those of you who don't know, chair flying is much like an actor rehearsing lines and body movements before acting a scene, or a basketball player with eyes closed visualizing defeating a defender to take the jump shot in open court and sinking the ball into the net. I have always found chair flying closely akin to daydreaming, which as a child and an adult I do quite often.

Aviators call it chair flying because they will literally sit in a chair in front of a mockup of the cockpit and go through all the actions and radio calls that they expect to make in any given flight. They will even touch the switches in the correct order as they progress through their faux flight. It is a powerful technique to build muscle and mental memory to assure a smooth flow in the cockpit and make their actions second nature. Having the confidence that chair flying builds makes the actual flight seem like second nature—even if the flight has never actually been flown before.

The basis of this book that you hold in your hands originated from chair flying—well, visualization, more precisely.

In the beginning of my real estate career I would lie awake in bed at night fretting over the meeting I had scheduled for the

Seth Wilson flying with the Alaska Air National Guard to Cold Bay from Anchorage on a routine training mission.

next day, the property inspection that had some bad findings on a building I had under contract, or the loan I just signed for with full-recourse.

I would worry myself to insomnia by imagining all of the potentially bad or negative outcomes that could possibly happen. Rather than be a victim of my own anxiety, I would create one-line solutions as to how I would eliminate the risk or cure the challenge if the bad event ever did occur. Through experience I later learned that most of the horrible events that could happen never do—and they are even more rare if appropriate actions are taken to head them off at the pass.

Within these one-line solutions I started to hear many sayings from my Air Force experience echo in my head: fly your own plane first, fight for centerline, and other words of wisdom that I share with you in this book.

Once I had a good one-line solution, I would then build the steps that I would take to relieve the possibility of ill fortune befalling me. I would write these steps down on the notepad in my phone, and I would give the note a good headline so I would always be able to find the list when I needed to use it.

One such example is "Items required from the seller before the start of the due diligence period." Not very exciting, I know, but descriptive. Later when I bought my second property, I referred to the list I had made when I purchased my first property. Since there were new things I learned or a slightly different set of circumstances, I would expand on the list and the list has since expanded every time I have bought another property. It was very clear to me that I was building a checklist (I've explained my checklist system in an earlier story) that fit into a larger system of systems.

What I later acknowledged about my sleepless actions was that I was chair flying scenarios before they happened. I was preparing myself, my vendors, and my team for success by not making snap, knee-jerk reactions but by having a well-thought-out plan that I could use as solid footing to jump forward from.

Why Chair Flying Works

I became 100 percent sold on the concept of chair flying while I was in pilot training at Laughlin Air Force Base, Texas. In my pilot training class a couple of students were struggling with one of the most intense and rigorous portions of training. The challenge that they seemed to have was that the fire hose effect in the cockpit was simply overwhelming them (I explained the fire hose effect earlier in this book). They could perform any one action to standards, but they were just having trouble performing all of the actions all at once.

The "fire hose" list included talking on the radio, scanning for traffic, keeping their plane within tight flight parameters, navigating, and staying within the proper airspace. This is just a small portion of what was occurring all the while the flight instructor in the backseat was quizzing them about everything that they could ever hope to know about flying the T-6.

Many people in the general public would just throw their hands up right before they threw in the towel. Not these two officers. They got serious about chair flying. I would watch them sit down with a notebook and in longhand write out every single action from the time they stepped up to the airplane until the time they unstrapped from the ejection seat. Literally hundreds of actions had to be executed the Air Force way. They filled numerous notebooks with this disciplined approach. I was amazed by their dedication to their training and the Air Force.

I was not the only one who took notice. The instructors did too. I overheard that the instructors were impressed by the students' techniques and noticed a significant improvement in their flight performance in the following weeks. Why? Because these students had already "flown" the mission before it happened.

Chair Fly Your Business

Flying is expensive. Real estate is expensive. Business in general is expensive. There is no reason to add to the cost of doing business because of lack of preparation or not fully understanding the desired outcome or actions to make the outcome a reality.

I found myself working in the Air Force for a brief stint at Scott Air Force Base, Illinois, home of Air Mobility Command (AMC) and just minutes from my childhood home, developing the command's way forward on a new and very expensive tactical datalink system. AMC is responsible for the worldwide operation of the Air Force's cargo and air refueling airplanes. Working there was exceedingly boring due to the massive layers of bureaucracy and lack of action, and on top of it all, I was the low man on the totem pole so my opinions didn't count for much.

What I did glean from my time at AMC was that this huge engine of military might chair flew. This is a great example of how chair flying can go from the flight line to the boardroom. Let me explain.

While the generals and other high-level officers and government contractors didn't sit in front of a mockup of a cockpit, they would have what is called Course of Actions (COAs). An expert in a given field would give a PowerPoint presentation on the paths that a project could take and the resulting desired outcome as well as any unfavorable outcomes.

Normally, three separate COAs were developed and presented with all the steps to execute the project, the cost, any other pertinent facts, and the positive and negative effects of all three. There would then be a discussion, and the decision maker would then choose one COA to proceed with. More accurately the decision maker, normally a general, would want to put his own spin on the COA, just so he could get his stink on it, and the decision was made for the rest of us to execute.

This military discipline and practice extended from when these general officers were low-level lieutenants. The generals knew that chair flying worked because they had practiced the art for many years and stuck with a good thing all the way to the highest echelons of the military.

Turning Skyward

Before my daydreams turned skyward, I lived the life of a normal kid in Belleville, Illinois.

"Hey, Mom, wanna bike ride across the state of Missouri with me next summer?" my eleven-year-old self asked her. I just gotten home from a Boy Scout meeting, and one of the scoutmasters who was into cycling pitched the idea to a group of dads and boys. Thinking that my father probably wouldn't be interested, I decided to ask my mom because she liked doing physical exercise things like this.

"Sure," she replied, probably thinking I would forget all about it.

Ten months later after as much preparation as a twelve-year-old and his scout troop could muster, we got on a train in St. Louis destined for the other end of the state, a station just outside of Kansas City. Our bikes were packed into a U-Haul and driven down I-70. It wasn't just us scouts and brave parents though; it was an organized ride of 400 or so other riders, many of which were cycling fanatics and had taken a week's worth of vacation to embark on this 350-mile trek on the back roads and state highways of the Show-Me State. We would cycle 50 to 80 miles a day and spend the nights in tents we erected in state parks. As a preteen this was an exciting new adventure. Now I prefer to camp in the local Marriott.

Seven days of peddling later, my mother and I arrived at the Mississippi River. We had completed the entire ride even when other scouts and their dads skipped a day to go on a float trip.

I had just become the youngest person to ever bike across the state of Missouri.

When the local newspaper asked me how I managed to keep pedaling for all those days and all those miles, I told them how I motivated myself. I would say, "Only five more miles, only five more miles." Little did I know then that I was simply visualizing myself riding for a short five more miles until I could get to the next state park to set up my tent.

My mom and I did this ride for the next few summers until I turned seventeen and visualized myself doing something else with my summer vacations.

Keep Sharp

There are any number of reasons that people or organizations don't chair fly. They may think it is silly, or not see much of a return from the act, or they could just be lazy.

The fact of the matter is that people who don't daydream, practice their craft, or take the initiative may very well have full and successful careers and businesses—but they will never be great. Yes, I understand that it is time consuming and, yes, I understand that it may feel or look goofy chair flying, but who cares?

My fellow students didn't care and they were in a room filled with sharp people and their big egos. They didn't care what others thought of them as they sat in the corner of the flight room and essentially did chants rocking back and forth studying their handwritten text. It certainly wasn't cool, but it was undoubtedly effective. It is in my opinion that without this chair flying technique, they would have been eliminated from training as opposed to flying around the globe as they do now.

Fully understanding the rules to the game and all the possible outcomes allows an individual and organization to seize opportunities when they arise (like I did as a young Boy

Scout by seizing the weak moment from my mother's decision-making) and overcome obstacles when they show themselves. There is no better way to capitalize on these actions than to take the time to simply chair fly and visualize the future.

LEADING WITH LESS EXPERIENCE

Surround yourself with the best people you can find, delegate authority, and don't interfere as long as the policy you've decided upon is being carried out.
—Ronald Reagan

El-Tee what's the plan for the rest of today?" a technical sergeant with more than fourteen years of military service asked me.

"Well, the colonel told me to not make any decisions, so let's call it a day," I replied.

With that announcement two noncommissioned officers and a secretary packed up their things, got up from their desks, and walked out the door. I stood there slightly dumbfounded as I was mostly joking when I suggested that we should leave the office four hours early.

It was an early Friday afternoon in the spring of 2006, and I was a brand new second lieutenant. I had commissioned as an officer just a month or so prior, and I now outranked 80 percent of the US military.

On this specific day I was left in charge of the small detachment as the rest of the officers were either on leave or performing temporary duty off site. The week prior in the staff meeting, the commander of the Reserve Officer Training Corps (ROTC) detachment, where I was retained as cadre after having completed the ROTC training and graduating college myself just months earlier, told me in jest: "Well, El-Tee (a shortening of my rank at the time of lieutenant abbreviated as LT), it looks like you are in charge next Friday so don't make any decisions, okay?"

He said this in jest but also knew that I could get the detachment and myself in precarious situations with almost no prompting at all. You see a few weeks earlier there was the small incident of me parking a borrowed Army Humvee on the front lawn of a Hooters restaurant to impress the waitresses. The stunt was only mildly successful.

"Sure thing, boss," I replied as I glanced around the room at the other cadre that was made up of three other officers, two enlisted personnel, and one university-provided secretary.

That's when I first realized that what I was taught in the preceding four years of officer training was a reality. With no certifications, with no military experience outside of training, and with no measurable time in the uniform, I had taken an oath to lead those with less rank and follow the orders of those with higher rank—and so had everyone else in the military. I could at any time be legally in charge and responsible for a whopping 80 percent of the military force as the lowest ranking officer in the Air Force.

This is possible because most of the military personnel are enlisted and known as noncommissioned officers (NCOs). These NCOs are the privates, the airmen, and the sergeants of our fighting force. They are technical experts in their career fields and willingly follow the orders of the leadership structure established above them. All officers regardless of rank or time in service are placed above the enlisted in the rank and leadership structure. I recognized my awesome and humbling responsibility.

Right away the conflicts and errors that may arise from this structure are visible. How is a know-nothing lieutenant who can barely wear his uniform correctly going to be able to lead and command NCOs with sometimes decades of experience and expertise in their profession?

The "El-Tee" may, in many cases, not even understand the job and technical skills of the NCOs, yet is still lawfully in charge of the situation, is directly responsible for the outcome, and must make decisions that he may not fully understand. On top of all of this it is within our customs and courtesies for the NCO to call the twenty-one-year-old officer "Sir" and to salute him, the same way he would any other officer including generals!

There is certainly a delicate balance that must be struck going forward. First, with all credit going to the NCOs, they are some of the most patient people that you ever come across when it comes to working with a new officer. They understand the structure and they understand the cooperate-to-graduate slogan. They know that the failure of the officer is a failure of the whole organization, and there is nothing to be gained from allowing another to fall, especially when they could have stopped or changed the actions that led to the result.

I often think of the NCOs treating the new lieutenants as puppies. They have to learn the rules and how things are done, so a gentle and consistent mentorship has to occur in the relationship. In return, the officer has to be willing to accept this type of guidance and not get hung up on the rank structure. The newly minted officer must also be willing to ask dumb questions and constantly be on the hunt for new information and techniques.

The officer has to have a clear understanding that they know nothing about everything without giving up their authority. A fine line must be walked here. "In my experience" is a phrase that should not come out of a lieutenant's mouth—ever—or else they risk the fate of hearing the sound of moans and the sight of eyes rolling in the heads of the people that they lead.

But since I haven't been a lieutenant in more than eight years, I can say this: In my experience the new officer should give the objective to his NCOs and the overarching plan of action and let them conclude how to get from where they are to where the objective is. As a commanding officer once told me, "I am not going to tell you how to bake the cake, Seth, I just know how I want it to taste. The rest is up to you."

Allowing the NCOs to come to their own plan of action, with their decades of experience, is always a great way for a new officer to learn the process and lets them lead as opposed to manage. It is then the officer's responsibility to approve, deny, or modify the plan of action, but with the newfound experience, he should feel comfortable and confident going forward.

Knowing Nothing about Everything

While this is very military centric, it applies to any situation in the civilian world as well. As a matter of fact it happens to me now in real estate nearly daily. How? Well I don't want to work with people with less experience or who are less capable than I am. That won't help me grow or expand. I am always looking for the smart individuals who have been there and done that, whether that be in banking and finance, construction and development, marketing and sales, or management.

I am constantly sitting down at the head of the table with groups of highly skilled (and well paid) professionals who are looking to me for guidance and answers regarding how we will move forward and make successes of our projects. Let me tell you, I know very little about law, accounting, taxes, or any number of other professional subjects—but I know the people who do! Then

I do everything I can to earn their respect through my leadership style and willingness to learn and act on their advice.

So while developing these leadership skills takes finesse and many years of experience, the core principles were being taught to me on that Friday afternoon more than a decade ago. Looking back I should have asked the NCOs what they had done in other situations like this in the past, and what they thought we should do in this situation rather than pretending that I had all the answers. I should have asked if they had other work that they could be doing or if there were any other projects we could get ahead on. That would have been the prudent and responsible course of action.

But let's get real. I would have dismissed them early anyway; after all, I was only a lieutenant.

My Mother Was a Lieutenant

My father was an only child and on the front wave of baby boomers, having been born in 1946. My fraternal grandparents worked hard and were savvy with the money that they did make. They rented rooms to students and tourists at the University of Illinois in Champaign-Urbana and, in an interesting foreshadowing to my entry into real estate, also rented trailers.

Their real financial break came when they sold their first house and invested the proceeds in the long-term booming stock market and more conservative CDs, which were making good returns themselves then. My grandparents were diligent with their money because they had worked so smart and hard to earn it.

My father is highly educated with two masters degrees, and he put them to good use through his young adult life working with inner city high school students in East St. Louis, Illinois, as a biology teacher and then with explosives—also managing the safety that is required in that line of work in the coal mines of southern Illinois.

My mother's path was not as easy. A strong, single mother raised her in the 1950s and 1960s when such family arrangements were not the norm. Mom was the youngest of three and the only girl. When she was still quite young, my grandmother snatched her children from school, in a clandestine operation, and ran. No one knew of her plan until she showed up in the middle of the night with three small children at the doorstep of a distant relative in rural Missouri. You see my biological grandfather was a champion boxer in the state of Texas. The problem was he didn't know when to stop swinging.

My maternal grandmother had been raised during the Depression, so needless to say nothing of hers went to waste. Being a single mother in the fifties and sixties was no easy task. My grandmother worked steadily and proudly in hourly jobs. If her kids needed new shoes, she didn't have the means to go out and buy them; she would have to save the money, possibly for weeks while her growing kids wore shoes too small, until the money was there so they could get shoes that were appropriately sized.

My mother was also well educated with a master's degree. She commissioned into the Air Force in the 1970s when, as my tough-as-nails grandmother told her, the only women in the military were "lesbians and whores." My mother being neither ignored her mother's comments and earned her commission as a second lieutenant. She worked in public affairs, the military equal opportunity office, and finally held the prestigious position of inspector general, where only those of the highest integrity and judgment worked.

My parents were introduced by my father's college roommate who also worked with my mother at Scott Air Force Base. They were married in 1982, and, in 1984, baby (me) made three, and they moved to southern Illinois shortly after my first birthday in 1985. By then, my father was an executive for Belleville Shoe Manufacturing—the largest supplier of combat boots to all branches of the military. The company also had civilian sales.

In my high school years when my mother had risen to the rank of Lieutenant Colonel in the Air Force Reserve, the family joke was that my dad made the boots and my mom kicked ass in them!

GO AROUND

I think it's very important to have a feedback loop, where you're constantly thinking about what you've done and how you could be doing it better. I think that's the single best piece of advice: constantly think about how you could be doing things better and questioning yourself.
—Elon Musk

So there I was flying in southern Arizona in a two-ship formation; we were staying in position as good wingmen do. At this phase of flight my crew was becoming fatigued with the long mission, and we had begun to have low confidence in the aircraft leading us (flight lead) on the low-level route.

The mission required us to fly our 120,000-pound aircraft 300 to 500 feet above the ground and deep into valleys to hide from enemy radar—then pop up at the last minute, open the back of the plane, and allow two pallets of much-needed supplies to fall out of the airplane under the equipment's rigged parachute. Then we were to get close to the ground again to egress the simulated combat zone and save ourselves.

Having followed the leader through a number of simple and advanced maneuvers, we determined that the pilot ahead of us wasn't as confident in himself and his flying as he should have been. We came to this conclusion because of the way that he had been leading the formation and the nonstandard radio calls that came from the aircraft in front of us. The leader's lack of confidence rubbed off on my crew about having confidence in him and his leadership abilities.

At the end of the two-hour mission, we were done with all of the dangerous, high-risk flying. All we had to do now was a formation landing. No big deal.

As we criticized the pilot in front of us, we executed the appropriate checklists and prepared for landing.

"Landing gear," the flight engineer called out per the checklist.

"Down. Indicator checks. Pilot," the pilot flying to my left responded.

"Down. Copilot," I sang in response.

The checklist was complete and we were cleared to land, easy. Three hundred feet off the ground in the descent to the runway, at that time I was investigating the noise myself, the pilot asked, "Why is the gear horn still on?"

My eyes raced to the landing gear indicator, which the pilot and I both verified was down and the handle was down, but the landing gear indicator was in fact in the up position.

"Crew. Going around!" the pilot declared, as he pushed the throttles forward greatly increasing the noise and the thrust from the four burly 4,590-shaft horsepowered turboprop engines.

Go-Around Thoughts and Execution

One of the first things all pilots are taught is to be ready for a go-around and how to safely execute the maneuver.

In the C-130 it's ingrained in my mind and muscle memory because I have chair flown it and practiced the maneuver numerous times:

1. Advance throttles as required to establish safe airspeed and the appropriate climb profile.

2. When appropriate airspeed, altitude, and climb profile are established, direct the PM (pilot monitoring) to set/ check flaps 50%.

3. Direct the PM to raise the landing gear when certain that the airplane will not be touched down (as required).

4. After the above procedures have been accomplished, proceed as though from a normal takeoff.

A go-around is a procedure that is performed if a pilot is not completely satisfied that the prerequisites are in place for a safe landing. A go-around is a standard maneuver that discontinues an approach or landing. Go-arounds are designed so that if the crew finds themselves in a precarious or potentially dangerous situation, they may simply refuse to accept the circumstances and try again.

It is in my opinion that learning how *not* to land should be taught first to any student pilot regardless of experience, even before they are taught how to actually land. While this statement may seem confusing or paradoxical, please stay with me.

Go-arounds are a commonly taught maneuver and are practiced by all disciplined pilots, whether they are brand new to aviation or have thousands of hours of flight time. To this day I still practice go-around procedures, as do all my fellow Air Force pilots.

Why Perform a Go-Around

Go-arounds are a normal part of the business of flight. It is a basic and easy-to-use tool for pilots to ensure that safety is not compromised during the approach and landing phase of flight.

The reasons for a pilot to execute a go-around are seemingly endless, but one of the more exciting if not less practical conditions occurs when a bus full of nuns pulls out onto the runway. To avert tragedy, the pilot must immediately go around or risk disaster. In this dream sequence, the pilots are once again the heroes of the skies and saviors of humanity all in one maneuver.

A more realistic list but certainly not an all-inclusive list of the reasons for a go-around are these:

- The aircraft is not within the parameters to land. This is also called a stabilized approach. A stabilized approach considers aircraft configuration, speed, energy state, height above the ground at various stages of the approach path, power settings, and rate of descent.

- Loss of communication or vague instructions from the air traffic controllers.

- Before-landing checklist is not complete.

- Potential conflict with other air traffic or aircraft and vehicles on the runway—the most common reason in my experience.

- Weather: wind speeds and gusts, turbulence, visibility, and cloud layers.

Some of these reasons to go around are written in stone such as the visibility and cloud layers or the parameters of a stabilized approach. Others, however, are completely up to the pilot's judgment and good sense.

Be Prepared

Like all things in life there are always consequences to actions to include taking the appropriate course of action if a go-around is required. Pilots may not be ready to go around. Pilots often focus so much on the landing that the thought of an alternative may not have entered their mind, so when they do need to execute a go-around, they aren't prepared.

During a go-around, a number of moving parts can disorient an unprepared pilot. The pilot could possibly lose control of the aircraft or cause a conflict with another airplane flying in the area. In some rare, but documented, cases a pilot may become so disoriented due to lack of preparation that he flies the airplane that is fully under his control into the side of a mountain.

Real Estate Go-Around

Thinking about going around in real estate is really simple. I am always ready to go around and try again. If on the other hand I think that I *have* to land (close the deal), I *have* to complete this objective, I *have* to have a great fiscal year, I have to have more marketing, I *have* to have more X, Y, or Z, I will just set myself up for failure. The challenge is that sometimes the sun and the stars and the moon do not align to make goals happen.

I have to be ready to say, "Hey, you know what? This is a good try. We are going to continue to attempt to meet our goals; however, at this time we are going to go around, we're going to re-attack. We are not going to meet our objective so at this instant we aren't going to pressure ourselves into a bad situation."

It's rare to have the discipline to say, "I don't like the terms of this loan and I'm not willing to accept them." To say, "We did the property inspection and there are some issues and the issues need to be worked out." Even though there may have been months of work into the property prior to purchasing, even though there may have been tens of thousands of dollars spent on inspections and other fees, if it is the day of the closing and there's something not fundamentally sound about the deal or it's just not going to work, just say, "I'm going to go around."

Will that cost you the deal? Maybe it will, but it is much better to lose a few thousand bucks and a couple of months of time to find that a property will not work for the plan than to spend millions of dollars of investors', lenders', and my own money to find out that this property is not going to work for us in a few years because we forced the deal to happen. This is in the same vein that a pilot might force an airplane to the ground because his ego can't stand to not land on the first try.

I would much rather have no property than a bad property.

Same thing with tenants. I tell this to the leasing agents too: "We would rather have no tenant than a bad tenant. Don't let occupancy and vacancy goals put pressure on you to move people in who do not meet our requirements or that you think will not be a good fit for this property."

If we have a goal of being 95 percent occupied by the end of a sixty-day term, the last thing we want to start doing is putting high-risk tenants in the property because the bad tenants are going to attract more bad tenants and they're going to scare away all the good ones. If the leasing manager tells me, "Seth, we couldn't make our leasing goals because we had issues with the tenant quality or applicant quality," no harm, no foul, literally and figuratively on that end.

If we start moving in tenants who, after two or three months, stop paying rent, start causing conflicts with the good tenants, start damaging the property, I am going to have a serious discussion with the leasing agents about what's going on and why they did not set us up for a good approach and landing with the new move-ins. This is a good example of a go-around for the management leg to the three-legged stool.

On the acquisition leg of the stool, if there is a material challenge, I am not going to accept a property in a poor condition without a satisfactory resolution. Yes, we could lose the property because of our demands; however, I would rather tell my investors, "This property doesn't meet our strict requirements, and we will not be able to hit the target return if we are required to put in an additional $250,000 for repairs." I don't want to tell them a year later that there is a capital call for the money that we need to come out of pocket to meet the property obligations. This focus will create a trusting and long-term relationship as opposed to an investor who thinks that my firm and I are a bunch of circus animals.

All the money up front for inspections, earnest money, and other expenses comes out of my pocket anyway, so there is no loss at all to the investors. Even if the money is in the partnership account and the checks are ready to be signed, and I decide to go around on a property because of an issue, we will simply circle until we can come to a satisfactory resolution for all parties involved.

The investors I have worked with are always very understanding of my go-around ethos because I am showing a high level of discipline and maturity as opposed to pushing forward to the close just so I can collect my fees from them and then be stuck with a property that does not work, does not fit the business model, and will either cause, at best, mediocre returns, or at worst cause the loss of investor money. I have to have the discipline and fortitude to know that this is not my landing; we're going to go around, we're going to try it again. That philosophy has always played well for me.

Someone Made Me Do It

I often fly south of San Diego into Brown Field working with the Navy SEALs. Brown Field is generally a small airplane field, and the C-130 is a large airplane—a little miss-match in this instance. The C-130 has an approach speed of between 130 and 140 knots. The small airplanes like the Cessnas and Pipers and other single-engine piston airplanes have an approach speed of around 65 knots. So I am flying at about twice the speed that they are on final approach.

The air traffic controller cleared a much smaller aircraft to land in front of us, but did not give us the amount of space that we needed to land behind them. Because I was traveling twice as fast as the small Cessna, I needed twice the space that air traffic control would give another small aircraft in my position.

The Herk did not get the consideration that she required. The Cessna landed and did not clear the runway in time for me to make a safe landing behind him.

I said, "Crew, going around. Traffic." I followed the procedures:

1. Advance throttles as required to establish safe airspeed and the appropriate climb profile.

2. When appropriate airspeed, altitude, and climb profile are established, direct the PM (pilot monitoring) to set/ check flaps 50%.

3. Direct the PM to raise the landing gear when certain that the airplane will not be touched down (as required).

4. After the above procedures have been accomplished, proceed as though from a normal takeoff.

I went around and successfully landed after having a brief and semiprofessional discussion with the air traffic controller about spacing required for the C-130.

Make sure that if you do go around, you have good reason, and you can explain why. The people that you explain why to, if they get upset or angry with you, probably aren't the kind of people that you want to be working with. The people who respect your decision and understand why you did what you did—those are the types of people you want to work with in the long term.

Back in Southern Arizona

After the pilot called the go-around in the blazing Arizona desert, he followed the procedure:

1. Advance throttles as required to establish safe airspeed and the appropriate climb profile.

2. When appropriate airspeed, altitude, and climb profile are established, direct the PM (pilot monitoring) to set/check flaps 50%.

3. Direct the PM to raise the landing gear when certain that the airplane will not be touched down (as required).

4. After the above procedures have been accomplished, proceed as though from a normal takeoff.

(Notice that I have run through this sequence of events three times already. It is to reiterate how important it is to know how to go around and not be afraid to do it.)

The go-around was performed flawlessly.

As we troubleshot our situation, we were confused. The pilot called for the gear to be put down and I did. The gear handle was in the correct, down position, but the landing gear were still in their wells. At the pilot's command I recycled the landing gear—nothing—the gear were still up and had not even tried to move. So we ran a new checklist I named "the wheels won't come down checklist."

As we progressed through all the reasons why the landing gear would not come down, we found that the circuit breaker controlling the electrical motor of the landing gear had either popped or been accidentally pulled out during our aggressive maneuvering. In some rare instances when there is a lot of movement of pilots or other crew members, articles of clothing or other items such as bags will snag a breaker and pull it out. This is what we believed happened in this scenario.

Had the pilot not executed the go-around, we would have landed on the belly of the airplane. Our landing roll would have gone from about 4,000 feet to 400 feet!

Every year airplanes land with the gear up either from forgetting to put them down or mechanical reasons. While this is not normally a fatal event, it does make for good news headlines and pictures, and it makes for bad endings to careers if the landing gear was left up due to the fault of the aircrew.

In the end the airplane told us that something was wrong with the blaring gear horn, and we used good teamwork and the checklist to find the source of the issue and correct it before something went really, really wrong.

There is no shame in a go-around. There is shame in a bad landing, or even worse a hard landing that causes damage to the aircraft (your property) or hurts somebody (lose money). You always have to land, but you don't have to do it right now.

FLY YOUR OWN PLANE FIRST

The competitor to be feared is one who
never bothers about you at all, but goes on
making his own business better all the time.
—Henry Ford

With barely enough brain power to be able to fly my plane around an unfamiliar airfield, in an unfamiliar aircraft, and doing my best to keep the right side of the plane up, I realized that the fire hose effect was on full blast.

I was reaching deep into my learning toolbox to try my best to remember what I am supposed to do at any specific point in time. As soon as I executed the proper steps or made the right radio call, something else would come up just as fast. I felt as if I was playing whack-a-mole at more than 200 miles per hour. No matter how hard I hit or fast I was, another event would pop its head up for me to conquer.

After about a month of flying the plane, I realized that I could anticipate the events that were to happen in the order they would happen and then how to successfully complete each one. My proficiency was due to a large amount of chair flying and good old-fashioned repetition. As pilot training students, we would fly at least once a day and often twice a day on flights that were just over an hour in duration. No flight was just for fun. They all had syllabus requirements, and each flight progressed us to be better and better soon-to-be Air Force pilots.

With my newfound ability to predict the next event as well as my increasing comfort in the cockpit of the T-6, I was able to "get ahead of the aircraft." This ability is a sign of a skilled aviator. Getting ahead of the aircraft is a term used to describe that a pilot not only understands what is happening right now but also what will happen. Getting ahead of the aircraft can be just a few minutes ahead or many hours ahead depending on the type of flight and skill of the aviator and their familiarity with the flight environment.

Business professionals who get ahead of their business seem like oracles. They seem to have a crystal ball that never fails them. Often these people are described as having the Midas or golden touch. The truth of the matter is that they just have a very good understanding of their business and the environment that it lives in. It takes years to get to this level of ability, but it can be learned and honed if the individual realizes that this is a skill and not an innate ability.

As I became a more forward-thinking pilot, I started to get confident in my skill and knowledge. As I was flying around one day, I started to become anxious about what the other airplanes were doing in the flight traffic pattern around the air base. Before, I all but ignored them. I had become quite good at the basics of flying the T-6 and was now more interested in what the other planes in the pattern were doing. The air base had three runways with different traffic patterns at different altitudes for the three different types of airplanes being flown at the base. I was only concerned about the inside runway for the T-6s. There are five patterns and ways to approach the inside runway. The maximum number of planes in the traffic pattern was seven— all zipping around at 200 knots.

Then I realized that I was in fact a genius and could not only fly my plane but other planes too! By that, I mean I'd look as I'd fly around and see other aircraft, and I would try to figure out, "What is it that they're doing? What are they thinking? What's going on with that bank angle? Why are they flying where they are flying, doing what they're doing?"

This distraction was much to my detriment. While I had a decent grasp of the fundamentals, I was certainly not a flying ace. My scan of my flight instruments started to slow down resulting in lazy flying, so paying attention to my altitude, airspeed, and what I was to do next had become undisciplined, and my plane started to fly off course.

My instructor picked up on my more erratic flying and said, "Hey, you need to quit flying other people's planes and fly your own plane first."

I quickly realized that he was right. I had to trust that the other students knew what they were doing and would not interfere with my plane or trespass into my flight path. I had to trust that they would follow their procedures and that they trusted me to follow mine.

In everyday society we place an enormous amount of trust in one another. In business we must put a lot of trust in each other as well. We must trust that the plumbers, electricians, engineers, general partners, and lawyers are all doing their jobs properly. We must learn to work with others because there is no way we can do all of these jobs and tasks as an individual.

That is not to say that we blindly trust them in their words or actions: "trust but verify" is integral to working with other professionals. Imagine someone spending all of their time and resources to control every outcome that could possibly happen, especially when these outcomes are completely out of their hands; these people are "general managers of the universe."

These micromanagers never make it very far because they spend too much time flying other people's airplanes. They believe that what they are doing is helpful but in reality all they are creating is resentment against themselves from others, and they are not minding their own business first.

Quit the Position of General Manager of the Universe

The biggest way these managers get wrapped up in their universe mastering is when they become obsessed with the supposed competition. I say supposed competition because the easiest way to stumble is by tripping over your own two feet. Firms and companies are far more likely to fail because of what they have or have not done within their own fiefdom as opposed to the outside invaders of the competition.

I never worry about what the competition is doing because they aren't on the same path as I am, and I need to do things my way not their way.

When the focus is inward rather than outward, a firm's performance will exponentially increase. Personally I am far more concerned about how my clients, tenants, and investors will be treated and the experience that they will have working with my firm.

For example, since we focus on our tenants' experience when they pay rent, we want to make it as easy as possible for the tenants to be able to pay us. We don't want to have any sort of resistance or obstacles that could slow them down from getting us the rent. If they say, "Well I was going to pay the rent, but I couldn't do it because I ran out of checks" or "I couldn't pay because the gas station I go to get money orders was closed," then we set them up then and there with an automatic payment plan that is either attached to a bank account or credit card.

This makes it as easy as possible for them to pay and greatly enhances the bottom line because we aren't dependent on them remembering to pay rent or having the equipment to pay (checks or money orders).

If we were concerned about how the apartment down the street has their tenants pay the rent, we would be taking our eye off our business and flying someone else's plane.

The same holds true with investors. Find out what the potential investors really want and then find out what the tenants in a given market space really want. Put the two together and create a really good balance and a great platform to start or continue a business. Don't spend too much time looking at what others are giving their investors regarding dividends or returns. Know exactly what the investor wants and how to make that possible by giving the customer or tenants exactly what they want—this is a true win-win scenario, a situation that a whole business can be centered around and one that you will be handsomely remunerated for.

Yes it is of note to know what others are doing in the market, but just don't spend much time trying to emulate them.

Keep your head up, look around the market, find opportunities, find the best practices, but don't keep looking over the fence at what the neighbor is doing. A lot of competition is not necessarily even real. Once the curtain is lifted, the public finds that some companies are all just smoke and mirrors. Think of Enron. Had Enron's competition gotten a hold of Enron's playbook, they would have quickly found out that Enron was a shell of the company contrary to what it was portraying itself to be.

This raises the question of how many other companies out there are also just blowing smoke. Not to say that all companies are being dishonest, but the amount of disorganization does surprise me, even within companies that are successful. So while the successful company does seem to be worth emulating, just be aware that they may not be as perfect as they seem.

In that same thread, you're dangerous if you're flying someone else's airplane because you're not flying your airplane. Plus there is no way to make money doing it. There's no profit in keeping tabs on what the property, the investor, or the owner down the street is doing unless you want to buy their property. There's no profit in watching other people build their successes or watch their failures, other than to learn a lesson or two from them. Even still, there's just no profit there. It's a waste of time and energy to be concerned about the guy across town who is building a new 300-unit high-rise luxury apartment, when that's not really even the space you are in.

When flying the airplane, consider only the three constant questions: What am I doing right now? Am I doing it well? Then what is going to happen next? Really just focus on what you're doing. Understand what's coming up next. That's the *next* most important thing.

These questions have subquestions to include: What's going to happen at the next waypoint? Which direction is the turn? What's the heading? Airspeed? Is there a checklist to be followed here? When will the aircraft get configured? Turn the lights on or leave them off? Is there a radio call to make? Is there a change of radio frequencies? What's next and then what's next?

If you're worrying about the other guy who's flying around you, you're not minding your own business and you don't know what you're going to do next. Events are going to fall through the cracks, people will fall through the cracks, and eventually money will fall through the cracks and either be lost or never come in at all. A whole lot of challenges will be caused that could otherwise be prevented by just minding your own business.

Sometimes firms and people will see others flying, and they'll have a little resentment toward them because they are acting as the general managers of the universe. I gave up on being a general manager of the universe many years ago. I did this for a selfish reason; it doesn't help me. I gain nothing from watching cable television. I gain zippo from participating in pop culture.

A lot of people think it's crazy that I don't read or watch the news. In fact, I don't really watch TV at all. It does not help my company or my family to learn that 100 people were shot in Chicago over the Fourth of July weekend. There is just no benefit there to me. Plus the world is a much safer place when you don't watch the news. I also don't watch TV because I spend my time reading and studying up on information I need to know to fly my own plane, literally, and run my own business.

Is this cold and distant of me? Sure is, but I really can only help so much; I can only listen to so many horrible stories before I just become numb to it all. I'll save my humanity for something I can actually affect.

SoCal Flying

I was recently flying out in California. The flight engineer who sits in between the pilots, and just aft of them, was obsessed about what other airplanes in the area were doing. It is very busy airspace in southern California, specifically between Tijuana and San Diego. He kept pointing his finger way out in front of us at all these airplanes, which is good. We're supposed to call out other planes in the area. We're supposed to understand that there are other aircraft in our airspace.

In addition to our eyeballs, we have electronic equipment that points out other aircraft. We also talk to air traffic control and build a situational mental picture in our minds of other pilots talking on the radio and stating their position. The flight engineer was just so obsessed with all these other airplanes flying around that he was not doing his checklist. We had to wait on him to get the checklist items done because he was so worried about other planes.

At one point I stopped and told him, "Hey, you really need to be flying your own plane. This is the plane that we're flying. We see them [the other aircraft] out there. We know that they're there. We're not going to hit them." And I mentioned the situational awareness, electronic equipment, and air traffic control.

"You really need to be working on what you have and what you're doing right now. We're falling behind because you're not getting your checklist done. That's going to cause us an issue because we're probably going to have to spend more time in the air, or we won't be prepared to land," I said.

He concentrated on what he needed to do. He got it done. The pilots did what they needed to do. Everybody was in their lane. Then we were all flying our own plane. We weren't trespassing on anyone else. We weren't worried about what other people were doing. Of course, we kept an eye on them to make sure that they did not trespass on us and get into our lane. Otherwise, everything worked out very, very well.

If you fly your own plane first, stay in your own lane, and mind your own business, you will succeed.

My Story

"It is easier for me to get you property if there is a story," the agent explained to me in a slightly condescending tone.

"What? A story?" Confused and slightly embarrassed. I told the real estate agent sitting across the table from me, "I want to buy an apartment building. I have my life savings to put into it along with every fiber of my being to make it a success."

"Well that's nice," he explained, "but no one knows you, you have very little money, and you have never bought property like this before. There is no way a reasonable seller would sell their property to you, and good luck getting a loan, you simply aren't qualified. So without a story, I can't help you."

I left the agent's office defeated and slightly demoralized. A story? What does that have to do with buying an apartment? And what story did I have to tell anyway?

This was the summer of 2013. The real estate market was recovering but only the most savvy of property owners knew it. The lending environment was hostile to say the least, and to compound my dilemma, I had little money, no apartment experience, and no one to show me the way. All I had was all the desire in the world, and a lifetime of people telling me that what I wanted to do wasn't possible—or at least not for me.

That's where my real estate story started, and this is where I am ending my book—for now—because I have gone on to write my own story and still have many, many decades of stories to live. If I had this book back in 2013 to hand to that agent, he now would know I had a great story to tell.

FINAL THOUGHTS

The future is limitless.
—Peter Thiel

I want to thank you for taking the time to read this book. Every word was specifically designed to add value to you and your company. I wanted the book to be easy to read and a book that could be read in just a few hours—so you can easily take it with you when you travel or as a light read before "lights out."

This book will be updated many times over the course of my real estate career. I am certain that even when I finally do retire from the business, sometime around my midsixties, more than thirty years from now, that I will add my last bit of wisdom—even if I will have fulfilled my twenty years of military service only nine years from now. I look forward to working with you and sharing this adventure in the decades to come.

I sincerely meant it when I said that I wanted you to be able to read this book and take away actionable items as well as start a relationship with you or your firm. Please feel free to reach out to me by email at Seth.Wilson@SierraWhiskeyProperties.com or by phone at (816) 307-0420 and please understand that when you leave a message, I will get back with you in less than twenty-four hours (and yes I do work on nights and weekends).

Visit us on the web at
www.SierraWhiskeyProperties.com.

EPILOGUE

Integrity, Service, Excellence

Integrity is the essence of everything successful.
—R. Buckminster Fuller

I ntegrity First, Service Before Self, and Excellence in All That We Do" are the core values of the United States Air Force. On day one of boot camp this motto is drilled into the ears, minds and eventually the very fabric of being of every airman and officer that will serve in the world's largest, greatest, and most lethal Air Force on the planet.

But these are more than just words; these values are a lifestyle. It is the baseline of trust and performance that every single uniform-wearing officer and airman is responsible for every day and for the rest of their lives. Any breach in this trust or this creed is reason for immediate dismissal and possible legal action being taken against the offender.

But how does this relate to real estate? Isn't the goal of real estate firms just to make money for themselves and investors? Isn't this military-grade ethos a little extreme for a company? Well let's break the parts of the core values down and explain each element, then bring them together as a whole to make your own conclusions on why the Air Force strictly follows and personifies integrity first, service before self, and excellence in all that we do.

Integrity First

I draw on the Air Force's *Little Blue Book* to shape these values for Sierra Whiskey so there is no room for misinterpretation of our values when it comes to employees, vendors, contractors, government officials, and investors.

Integrity is a character trait. It is the willingness to do what is right even when no one is looking. It is the moral compass—the inner voice, the voice of self-control, the basis for the trust imperative to any relationship.

Integrity is the ability to hold together and properly regulate the elements of a personality. A person of integrity, for example, is capable of acting on conviction. A person of integrity can control impulses and appetites.

But integrity also covers several other moral traits indispensable to business services:

- **Courage**. A person of integrity possesses moral courage and does what is right even if the personal cost is high. What comes to mind is some of the slick guys on Wall Street who have been accused of doing what is the most profitable, the act that will give them the biggest bonuses rather than the action that is right, just, or moral. Taking the quick or expedient path can be very tempting, but for me personally that I have always regretted it and taking the easy way out has left me sleepless too many nights—that is just one small reason why I always choose the action that I know is right all the way down to the core even if it is at a physical or fiscal cost to my firm or myself.

- **Honesty**. Honesty is the hallmark of the real estate professional because, in business, people's word must be their bond. Don't pencil-whip reports, don't cover up violations, don't falsify documents, and don't write or give misleading messages or reports. The bottom line is don't lie, and there can be no justification for any deviation. This is a very slippery slope as well. We all have seen time and time again, politicians, most notably, lie about an issue or get caught in a sticky situation rather than coming clean and admitting the error, mistake, or misrepresentation to cover it up. Often the cover-up is worse than the crime in the first place. The best way to cover up a lie is not to lie or make any misrepresentations in the first place.

- **Responsibility**. No person of integrity is irresponsible; a person of true integrity acknowledges his or her duties and acts accordingly. Most recently in the news a Japanese freighter hit a US naval ship. The captain of the ship was immediately relieved of his duty and command of the ship. He's probably going to lose his job, and his twenty-plus-year military career is essentially over because of this incident. Now is the captain at fault for the incident? The answer to that is probably no. He may not have even been on the bridge. While he did not command the ship in a reckless manner and he will most likely be found not liable, he is still responsible. That's what President Harry Truman meant when he said, "The buck stops here." The ship captain may not be the individual to blame for the incident, but he is the one responsible for the ship and her crew, and the buck stops with him.

- **Accountability**. No person of integrity tries to shift the blame to others or take credit for the work of others. No person can have responsibility without accountability and authority to make decisions, and there can't be accountability without responsibility. Sometimes the military and other organizations fail to realize that if someone is granted responsibility, they also are accountable but they must be granted the authority to act in the best interests of their responsibility. But one cannot have accountability without responsibility or authority for that matter—and round and round the logic goes.

♥ **Openness.** Professionals of integrity encourage a free flow of information within the organization. They seek feedback from all directions to ensure they are fulfilling key responsibilities, and they are never afraid to allow anyone at any time to examine how they do business. Openness may seem like it's a bit on the outskirts of integrity, but it is easy to lie to yourself without a free flow of information. If yes-men surround a leader, then the leader is misleading himself and his organization.

♥ **Self-respect.** To have integrity also is to respect oneself as a professional and a human being. A person of integrity does not behave in ways that would bring discredit upon himself or herself or the organization to which they belong. It is an all too common sight to see athletes, military members, politicians, and high-ranking CEOs of large corporations bring discredit upon themselves either personally or professionally, which then rubs off onto their organization. Violators often think that they can continue to lead the organization or be an integral part of their group. The reality is that they can't because they have shown that they are of low integrity. It makes people question both within and outside of the organization how they got to such a high level in the first place and what else is being mismanaged.

♥ **Humility.** A person of integrity grasps and is sobered by the awesome task of being a fiduciary and in the case of real estate firms managing the living space of numerous tenants and their families. A high-ranking military leader must understand that he is in charge of an awesome war machine, consisting of weapons and warriors. He must have humility to understand that many people's lives depend on his leadership and decision-making ability. He must remain humble and not get big headed about his position or authority, and not show his ego. Which will only cause him to misstep, take actions that are unacceptable or abuse the power position that he holds. The same is true for companies. They must realize that they have a duty not only to their shareholders but to society as a whole not just to themselves. Unfortunately, a number of both military and civilian leaders have been defeated by their own hubris.

These qualities are a great foundation and primer to what the Air Force officially believes integrity to be. However, there are all sorts of different definitions of what integrity is. There are numerous little cutesy quotes from people who try to explain what they believe integrity is or what it means to them, but what I'd really like to do is spend the time to discuss what I believe integrity is—and why it is the foundation of everything that I do.

If I ever hit rock bottom, I know that that rock bottom will be integrity, because that is what everything else that I do is built upon. Some people say integrity is a character trait—the willingness to do what is right, even when no one else is looking. Okay, so that's great. What does that mean? Integrity has all sorts of different facets, and I'd like to show how they relate to my day-to-day activities.

On a personal note, I once was caught in a lie. It was an untruth of a material factor. It was not a small one, and had I not confessed to my indiscretion I would probably not be writing this book today. It would have changed my life that much. And while it isn't necessary to discuss exactly what I did, just know that my indiscretion was something I should not have done and then, of course, tried to cover up.

I fully understand the damage to both an individual's reputation and psyche of not being a person of integrity. No one was hurt or injured, but it was a complete breach of character, and it was a turning point in my life personally on what integrity means to me. That's not to say that I still don't hedge the truth here and there to save the feelings of others, but anything of material nature, or fiscal nature, absolutely not. I strive to be as black and white as I can in this sometimes very gray world.

I expect that my team acts in the highest integrity, the people who work for me and work with me must also have the aforementioned traits. Sometimes when I have a first meeting with someone, I'm blunt about these virtues, and that's because I want them to fully understand what I do and what I expect from them. I work with the utmost of honesty, and I expect them in their performance with me to be the same. I believe this a very important part of integrity as well as being forthright.

So while you may not agree with some of these subpoints of integrity, for me personally this is at the core of my existence. I've built everything in my life, my family, and business upon integrity.

Service Before Self

Service Before Self tells us that professional duties to investors, lenders, and tenants take precedence over personal desires. At the very least it includes the following behaviors:

- **Rule following**. To serve is to do one's duty, and duties are most commonly expressed through guidelines, laws, and the intent of others (which will be grouped together as rules). While it may be the case that professionals are expected to exercise judgment in the performance of their duties, good professionals understand that rules have a reason for being, and the default position must be to follow those rules whether laid out by the US Securities and Exchange Commission (SEC), local or federal government, or other regulatory agency. The rules must be followed to maintain integrity, legality, and reputations.

♥ **Respect for others**. Service before self shows that a good leader and company place the investors and clients to include residents ahead of their own personal comfort or wealth. We must always act in the certain knowledge that all persons possess fundamental worth as human beings. Some landlords conveniently forget respect for others, such as their tenants. When times get tough, they may coerce or flat out lie to tenants about payments, security deposits, or maintenance. Or individuals such as Bernie Madoff will simply pocket investor funds for his own benefit. He is now learning his lesson on respect for others as he spends the rest of his life in prison.

The bottom line is this: a company must always place itself in the last place position. When a firm does their job as they say that they will, everyone will win—everyone—lenders, investors, tenants, vendors, and the firm itself. If there are temporary setbacks, the firm must be the first to add more capital if needed, and the last to get paid. This aligns the firm's interests with the project. Be proud of the ability to have the discipline and ability to take this stance.

A final thought: all companies are built to serve a need. Make sure that the need is being fulfilled 100 percent with service before self, and revenue will never be a challenge.

Excellence in All That We Do

Excellence in All That We Do directs the development of a sustained passion for the continuous improvement and innovation that will propel the company into a long-term, upward spiral of accomplishment, performance, and profitability.

♥ **Product/Service excellence.** Successful real estate firms must provide services and generate products that fully respond to investor and tenant wants and anticipate investor and tenant needs, and it must be done within the boundaries established by the firm's core values.

♥ **Personal excellence.** Real estate professionals must seek out and complete professional education, stay in physical and mental shape, and continue to refresh their general educational backgrounds. The best way to accomplish this is through reading pertinent information in books, articles, and websites; joining and attending a variety of professional organizations; watching webinars and attending training seminars and conferences in person and around the country—it is recommended that all companies and executives do the same.

♥ **Resources excellence.** Excellence in all we do also demands that firms aggressively implement policies to ensure the best possible cradle-to-grave management of resources.

- **Material resources excellence.** Business professionals have an obligation to ensure that all of the equipment and property they ask for and use is essential. Even if this means the elimination of a number of non-essential line items. This will reduce overhead and allow for stronger cash flow and property valuation.

- **Human resources excellence.** Firms must recruit, train, promote, and retain those who can do the best job for you. People really are the most precious asset to any company.

♥ **Operations excellence.** This form of excellence is one of the most exciting points and the one that most outsiders see. This is also considered execution (see more in the story on war gaming). Operations excellence involves complete respect to the process on the every level and a total commitment to maximizing team effort.

A number of companies are out to do only one thing: make the managers and company executives wealthy. While they are pursuing a type of excellence, it is not the kind that is required of win-win scenarios. They are only out for themselves. Long-term successful companies pursue excellence across the board—from the lowest level of cleaning trash off of the properties, to the highest level of structuring partnerships for the maximum advantage to everyone involved. The truly successful are constantly going above and beyond for their tenants, investors, and lenders.

My Role Model

A lot of what I said in this story may seem like a do-gooder personality or that I am being a good little Boy Scout. And that is okay for others to think of me. The purpose of this story, beyond exposing the reader to the core values of the Air Force, is to make clear as a bell my stance on many issues that plague the corporate, political, and larger general population of America.

The Air Force espouses these values and ensures that all of her service members live up to them for a very good reason. The American public has charged the Air Force with a fatal mission: to kill people and destroy their equipment. There can be no doubt in any service member's mind that the person that they are flying as a passenger with, a pilot that they have never met and may never see, is living by the same set of moral values as they are. The passenger must know that the anonymous pilot is an officer of high standards both professionally and morally.

In the same breath the pilot must believe that the passengers, maintenance personnel, and cargo loaders are just as sharp because any breach in this trust could be horribly fatal to the good guys—because in the end we need each other.

- ♥ Imagine the uncertainly or fear that an investor may have signing a large amount of money to your firm without the assurance that you are a person of character.

- ♥ Imagine the tenant who doesn't believe that you will fix the running toilet or that you won't take the actions necessary to make the apartment community safe.

These hesitations no matter how small will be complete deal breakers, and they will never tell you why they didn't invest with you or why they didn't move in. They will tell you anything else other than "I don't trust you." Eliminate these fears by being a person of integrity, service, and excellence.

I take the values of a strong, trusted military force and make them my company's own. I can find no better role model to emulate than the Air Force and the power behind the words and actions that they enshrine.

ABOUT THE AUTHOR

Seth S. Wilson is a real estate entrepreneur and best-selling author. An eleven-year Air Force veteran, Seth served as a navigator and combat pilot in Iraq and Afghanistan. He continues to serve his country as a pilot of the C-130 Hercules as a member of the Missouri National Guard.

Seth Wilson commanding a C-130.

As founder and managing member of Sierra Whiskey Properties, Seth is passionate about sharing his unique message—to his investors and other business firms—that blends high-end real estate with his adrenaline-charged experiences as a combat pilot.

With his eyes always skyward, Seth has been a pilot since the age of sixteen and a real estate investor for more than ten years. He still enjoys flying small planes and lives with his wife, Dana, in Kansas City, Missouri.

www.ingramcontent.com/pod-product-compliance
Lightning Source LLC
Chambersburg PA
CBHW022041190326
41520CB00008B/671